St Brendan of Kerry, the Navigator

Dom athair is dom mháthair
Dónal agus Máire Ua Donnchadha
a thug dom a beith mórálach
as na glúnta a d'imthig romhainn

St Brendan of Kerry, the Navigator

His life and voyages

GEARÓID Ó DONNCHADHA

OPEN AIR

Published by
OPEN AIR
at Four Courts Press
7 Malpas Street, Dublin 8, Ireland
email: info@four-courts-press.ie
http://www.four-courts-press.ie
and in North America by
FOUR COURTS PRESS
c/o ISBS, 920 N.E. Hassalo Avenue, Suite 300, Portland, OR 97213.

ISBN 1-85182-871-0

A catalogue record for this title
is available from the British Library.

Printed in Ireland
by ColourBooks Ltd, Dublin

Contents

Personal note

On 2 August 1980, five of us left Connecticut on board a 41-foot sloop, *An tSíocháin*, to cross the Atlantic to Ireland. Our skipper was Bill Verity, a legend of the sea who had set a world record by crossing the Atlantic single-handed in a 12-foot boat, the *NoNoAlca*, built to a traditional Mayan design. On that occasion he made landfall in Tralee Bay and arrived in Fenit. Bill was an amateur maritime archaeologist who researched historical events and recreated them. One such event was the voyage of Captain Bligh of the *Bounty* who completed a remarkable 3,000 mile navigation across the southern Pacific after Christian Fletcher had mutinied, seized his ship and cast him loose with some loyal crew in the *Bounty*'s launch. Bill studied the records in the British museum, built a boat to the *Bounty* launch design, and, single-handed, followed Bligh's itinerary across the Pacific. (It is of little relevance to our story that in Tonga a local chieftain's daughter married him – such are the perils of single-handed voyaging.)

When he arrived in Fenit, Bill became intrigued with the story of Saint Brendan who was born locally. Once again, Bill did his research and decided that Brendan was not a fool; while he undoubtedly used the local *naomhóg*, or curragh, for his inshore travel, for offshore work he built and used a ship like the ones he was familiar with from seeing those of the traders who came to Barrow and Fenit from Wales, France, Spain and the Mediterranean. So Bill set to study once again, guided by Dr George Little, and worked on a 12th century design of wooden ship, believing, correctly, that ship design had changed very little in the six hundred years since Brendan's time. Bill built a 20-foot scale model of this ship and set out, again single-handed, for the Bahamas and Florida. After some adventures that would have beaten a lesser man, Bill arrived in the Bahamas after 126 days. Bill was a feisty character who did not suffer authority gracefully and when he was confronted by a local policeman he wasn't in the mood to be co-operative, particularly as he was on hands and knees. He was unable to walk due to the time he had spent at sea.

"Where did you come from?" asked the custodian of the law.

"Ireland", said Bill.

"Where is that?"

Bill pointed to the north-east. "Out there."

"How far?"

"5,000 miles" said Bill.

"Where is your crew?"

"I ate them."

So Bill was arrested and handcuffed by the policeman. He was led, still on hands and knees, up the walkway of the marina, lodged in jail for the night and brought into court next morning. On the bench, as it happened, was Judge John Bailey of Tralee who knew Bill well.

"Great God, Verity, what are you doing here?" asked the magistrate.

"Cannibalism, your Honour", said the policeman.

The magistrate struck the bench and said, "Case dismissed: get him out of here!"

I trust I may be forgiven for this somewhat long digression which gives some idea of Bill Verity's character. We had an adventurous crossing during which a hurricane caught up with us and introduced us to the Atlantic in all its destructive power. We can thank Bill Verity for our survival. I also thank him for what he taught me about the sea and the people who travel upon it. I realize that of those who read about Brendan and his associates, the vast majority have no understanding of two things.

First, the need of some people to go to sea; the hunger to be away from land, to go where one will, at one with the ocean. Secondly, only those who have experienced the black moods of the ocean, the terrifying elemental power of wind and sea, only they can really understand what sea-going is about, only they can really understand people like Verity and Brendan.

Experiencing a major Atlantic storm is to meet nature gone mad. The visual element is overpowering. What I can best liken it to is to being among the Himalayas except that the mountains are moving, not regularly, but criss-crossing one another in tumultuous frenzy, running one across the breaking, white-foamed tops of others so as to hit the boat broadside and shake it like a terrier might shake a rat. Rising and falling in 40-foot waves every nine seconds leaves one entirely breathless and it takes every ounce of energy just to stay with the boat.

The blown, freezing spray is dashed into one's face at up to 100 knots. One lives in a virtual white-out, stung and blinded by spray, unable to predict the next movement of the boat. Worst of all must be the auditory cacophonous assault that limits the ability to think. Indeed, my most enduring memory is the noise of the storm. Bad as it is on deck, below it sounds as if the boat is coming apart. One becomes painfully aware of the stress on mast and rigging and one's faith in the products of human hands is tested severely.

Finally, the harassment and brutalization of one's senses enters into one's very consciousness so as to create a virtual out-of-body experience where one is bereft of all but the experience of the moment. Relatives, friends, familiar land places are no more. They are stripped from your consciousness, There is only you and the forces of nature. You have been stripped of civilization, of culture; you are left with the most primal instinct of survival. In this state you are one with the first human beings that tried to make sense of a new existence into which they had been thrust. Those who have weathered sea and storm are not the same again.

Since that day at the end of August 1980 when we arrived, shaken and bruised, in Fenit, I have sailed the waters that Brendan knew. I have gone to Inishnee and Inish Glora on the west coast of Ireland, to Iona, Barra, the Hebrides, the Orkneys, the Faeroes and Brittany. Brendan's mark is on all these places and on many more, as we shall see. Bill Verity died quietly in Listowel Hospital in 1988, a peaceful end to a turbulent life, a life lived to the full. Bill's grandmother was from Asdee on the Shannon; he had the spirit of Brendan, a fellow Kerryman.

Gearóid Ó Donnchadha

An Fhianait, Co. Chiarraí
16ú Bealtaine, 2004
Lá Fhéile Bhreanainn

Preface

As we ushered in a new millennium in the year 2000, we found ourselves in the best of times and in the worst of times. Economically we were in good shape (or so it seemed at the time) with the Celtic Tiger in full spate. Politically, things seemed good with the Northern peace process providing hope at last. Spiritually and morally it was a different story. We had become distanced from our roots, from the values that had made us the people we were. Individualism was over emphasized at the expense of neighbourliness and unselfish community involvement.

Crime rates burgeoned, especially violent crime, rape, murder and attacks on older people in their own homes. Addiction to drink, and the new phenomenon of binge drinking, the consequent carnage on our roads, and the increase in suicide and other forms of destructive deviance had become a feature of our lives. Child abuse, and its cover-up, particularly on the part of religious, caused great distress.

It was against this background that a group of people in Fenit, County Kerry embarked on a project to honour St Brendan of Fenit, St Brendan exemplified all that was best in the values of commitment to God and to one's neighbour. His courage in facing the perils of the sea made him the best-known saint of the early Middle Ages. The honouring of Brendan would be in two parts. The erection of an appropriate monument and the dedication of a heritage centre to the life and times of Brendan.

After some difficulty, planning permission was received for a twelve-foot statue on a four-foot plinth to be placed on the summit of Samphire Island at the entrance to Fenit harbour. The heritage centre will follow on. Tighe O Donoghue of Glenflesk, Killarney, an internationally acclaimed artist and sculptor, is sculpting the statue, in bronze. As we look forward to the erection of the statue in 2004, the local committee is fundraising to meet the cost of the project and is meeting solid support locally and elsewhere. We are especially grateful to the Harbour Board for making such a splendid site available.

What follows is an account of Brendan's life and travels. The book is in two parts. Part 1 gives an overview of Brendan's life and times, his missionary journeys, his founding of monasteries and his famous voyages. We have more knowledge of Brendan than of almost any other Irish saint; however, we must always keep a healthy question mark in our minds about everything we read. We will tell the story according to the best historical opinion and spare the reader a plethora of 'perhaps' and 'maybes'. This first part will be, of necessity, succinct, because of the nature of the second part. We will include, mainly, material that is not treated in part 2.

Part 2 gives a translation of the Irish *Life of Brendan* contained in the Book of McCarthy Reagh (or the Book of Lismore as it is better known) followed by some extracts from the Latin *Life* that is probably of the mid-ninth century. The original of this Latin *Life* is found in the *Codex Armachanus* in Marsh's Library in Dublin. It seems to be a translation, in great part, of the Irish Life, relating the same incidents in much the same order. However, the Irish Life, as we have it, finishes after Brendan's first voyage and tells us nothing of Brendan's later life. So we give a translation of extracts from the Latin Life that detail incidents of Brendan's later life. We also include a translation of the *Navigatio Sancti Brendani Abbatis* taken, principally, from a manuscript in the National Library in Paris, collated with certain Vatican and other manuscripts by the Most Rev. Patrick Moran in his *Acta Sancti Brendani* (1872).

PART ONE

Brendan's life and times

As we have seen, we know of Brendan (or Bréanainn) chiefly from four sources – the Irish *Lives*, the Latin *Lives,* the Latin *Navigatio Sancti Brendani Abbatis* and many vernacular versions of his voyage in the emerging languages of Europe, collectively known as the *Voyage of Brendan*. We also know of Brendan from the frequent mentions of him in the lives of other saints and in the many calendars and martyrologies that have survived in Ireland and in Scotland. One of the earliest references to Brendan we find in Adomnan's *Life of Colmcille*, written in 697. This latter work, written in praise of Colmcille, mentions Brendan's meeting with Colmcille, on Hinba, and says of Brendan "He was the greatest founder of monasteries of them all." An even earlier reference is in the poem of St Cuimin of Conor (Coindire) who sets out the characteristics of the Irish saints about the year 650. He says of Brendan:

Carais Brenainn buanchrabudh
Doreir shenuid is shamhaidh;
Secht mbliadne ar drium in mil mhoir

Ba docair in coir chrabaidh.

Brendan loved lasting devotion,
According to his synod and equals
Seven years on the back of the
    whale;
Severe was this mode of devotion.

The various sources of the *Navigatio* and the Latin *Lives* are in manuscript in all the major and many smaller libraries of Europe. The earliest source, the Irish Life, was probably written around AD 750 to 800, some two hundred years after the death of Brendan. The various editions of the *Navigatio* and the Voyages were the first and most popular reading material in the emerging languages of the early Middle Ages and inspired Dante in his *Divine Comedy* and Columbus in his voyage to the New World, as we shall see later.[1]

---

1 A full bibliography of sources and studies on the life of Brendan fills a substantial volume. A valuable book on the sources and subsequent studies of the Brendan material is Glyn S. Burgess and Clara Strijbosch, *The legend of St Brendan: a critical bibliography,* Dublin, Royal Irish Academy, 2000. One of the most insightful books on Brendan is Denis O' Donoghue, *Brendaniana: St Brendan the Voyager,* Dublin, Browne & Nolan, 1893. Though over 100 years old, it is well worth having, particularly for the extensive notes on matters local and further afield. Llanerch Publishers brought out a facsimile reprint of most of the book in 1994 under the title *Lives and Legends of Saint Brendan the Voyager.*

The *Voyage of Brendan* is a particular type of literature and is based on oral tradition of which we have manuscript evidence. This literature comprises *echtrae* (adventures), *fís* (visions) and *immrama* (voyages). The last of these are of the same genre as the *Iliad* and *Odyssey* of Homer, Virgil's *Aeneid*, Ovid's *Metamorpheses* and the *Arabian Tales* of Sinbad, some of whose themes they share. They require careful interpretation as we shall see.

It is difficult to separate myth and legend from fact, yet some things are fairly certain about the voyage of Brendan. Much research must yet be done to verify some of the points made below. To understand the *Voyage* one must see it as the weaving together of the secular life and travails of a seafarer and one's spiritual life as lived throughout the Church's year in union with Jesus Christ.

Overall, the *Navigatio* is a tour de force of imagination and symbolism exploring the limits of Christian doctrine and our relationship with God and the forces of good and evil that surround us. In, particular, the story of Judas gives us one of the first introductions to the idea of Purgatory which is very much an Irish innovation.

The idea of partial relief for those who did not immediately merit heaven is further explored in three further Irish tales. These are the *Vision of Fursey*, *the Vision of Tundal* and, most famous of all, *The Vision of Owen* in St Patrick's purgatory in Lough Derg. These three visions are extensions of the contents of the *Navigatio* and the visions of hell that Brendan enunciates. Indeed, Fursey was a relative and disciple of Brendan's.

Dicuil, an Irish monk, became astronomer and geographer at the court of Charlemange and published his work *De Mensura Orbis Terrae* at the beginning of the ninth century (*c*.825). His is the first written account of Irish hermits visiting Iceland and marveling at the midnight sun, in 795. Some think that this work may have inspired subsequent accounts of Brendan such as we have in his lives and voyages. On the other hand, it is more likely that Brendan or his associates in the sixth century were the founders of these communities.

Whatever may be said of the accounts of Brendan's voyages, it seems clear that, amidst the fantastic renderings of the saga, there is evidence that someone had experienced the ice floes of the north, the fog of Newfoundland, and the exotic birds and flowers of the Caribbean. It is not possible to prove that Brendan himself experienced the events of the *Voyage*, yet it is most likely, such was his reputation as a navigator, that his name came to be associated with the many undoubted voyages made by inhabitants of the coast of Kerry and of Ireland, so that in honouring Brendan we give honour to generations of Irish traders and fishermen who have braved the Atlantic and lived to tell the tale. Some, doubtless, went in search of the Promised Land, others went with missionary intent, many were blown long distances out to sea and off course and found themselves in the Faeroes, Iceland and places further afield.

Recent genetic research shows the same gene-pool in western Ireland, the Faeroes and Iceland. Further research will undoubtedly show that Irish sea-farers were in America a thousand years before Columbus. And they probably were not the first!

ORIGINS, BIRTH AND EARLY LIFE

The main features of the life of Brendan are well covered in part 2 of this book, in the *Life*, the *Vita* and the *Navigatio*, and there is no point in repeating what can be found there. We will concentrate mainly on matters that are not covered in part 2.

Brendan was born in 484 to Finlug and Cara in Alltraighe Cuille or Cin-beara, a district comprising the four miles from Spa to Fenit Island, some five miles west of Tralee in County Kerry, Ireland. Finlug was of the Alltraighe who were a sept of the Ciarraighe who have given their name to the present County Kerry. His mother, Cara, was of the Corca Dhuibhne of West Kerry. His most likely place of birth was Fenit Island, with Kilfenora, Tawlaught and Barrow also possibilities.

Brendan was born some nine years before the death of Patrick whose min-istry covered the North and West of Ireland and comprised the years 461 to 493. Finlug and Cara were pre-Patrician Christians. Christ was known in Ire-land as early as the second century. The early centuries saw much contact between the Continent, England and Ireland. Persecutions saw people finding refuge in Ireland from the earliest times.

We may be sure that many young Irishmen became Roman soldiers, as they later joined the armies of Britain, Spain, France and the Austrian Empire. Many of the Roman soldiers were Christian from early times. Others, like Sedulius and Caelestius, the associate of Pelagius, went from Ireland to Europe before AD 400. Sedulius, in Greece, wrote one of the greatest and most beauti-ful of our hymns, the *Carmen Pascale*, which begins '*A solis ortus cardine*'. Pelag-ius, of Irish descent, was opposed greatly by Saints Jerome and Augustine, but, *sin scéal eile*.

From 350 onward, bands of Irishmen pillaged Britain and France and brought back slaves, many of whom, including Patrick, were Christian. Later influences were people like Saints Ibar, Ailbe of Emly, Kieran of Cape Clear and Declan of Waterford who were influenced by travels in Wales and became Christian before returning to Ireland before 450.

A further influence, in the North, was Nennius' foundation at Whitehorn in Galloway in south-western Scotland in 397. Nennius was a disciple of St Martin of Tours who had founded the monastery of Marmoutier and ascetic monastery of Ligugé.

In 406 the Goths crossed the Rhine and in 410 sacked Rome. Many refugees must have come to Ireland from Gaul. In 410, also, Rome withdrew her army from Britain, allowing the Picts, Angles and Saxons to attack Wales and places like Whithorn – resulting in further refugees bringing the word of Christ with them to Ireland. Some Irish soldiers would have come home at this time, rather than follow the legions to Rome.

Prosper of Aquitaine, secretary to Pope Leo, wrote a Chronicle which contains an entry for 431: "Palladius was ordained by Pope Celestine and sent to the Irish believers in Christ as their first bishop." Many Irish were Christian at this time due to the evident faith and commitment of ordinary sailors, traders, travellers, refugees, slaves and even soldiers who came among them.

Palladius seems to have concentrated his apostolic efforts in the midlands and his dealings with the high king of Tara were later transferred to Patrick. This will be taken up in a separate chapter.

There seems to be some Coptic (Egyptian) influence that can only have come along the trade routes around the coast of Spain, France and Ireland. Alcuin, the Englishman, derided the work of Dicuil which we have already mentioned, criticizing him and his "Egyptian boys" who were mistaken in their computation of the date of Easter. This is another pointer towards the influence of the Eastern Mediterranean on Early Irish Christianity. The date of Easter was unique to the Irish in the western world and probably came from Eastern influence. The Irish early developed a taste for the wine of the East, for which they traded pelts and live animals and also the copper that was mined on the coasts of Cork and Kerry.

Fenit, near the mouth of the Shannon, was well known from prehistoric times. We find reference to Fergus of Fenit in a list of judges and scholars of the first century, in the *Senchus Mor*. For the next two centuries Fenit, or Fianan, was a favourite resort of the Fianna who may have given the place its name. We read in the Fiannaiocht of races on the "Strand of Barriman" (*Traig Bearamhain*, Barrow and Banna), and thence to Glenflesk and Caherbarna above Millstreet by way of Tralee and Killarney, and back again, with Fionn Mac Cumhal's black steed winning the race. Many *fulachta fiansa* (prehistoric kitchen middens) have been found, in this area, particularly around the back strand of Rahoneen "the lake where the foam on the billow's top leaps white". As the poet Oisin puts it:

> With weariness all weak and wan
> We reach the Strand of Barriman;
> The well-known path again we meet,
> And friends with eager welcome greet.

And, indeed, the *fulachta fiansa* testify to the celebrations that followed!

Fenit must have been a common port of call for travellers. Their boats and ships were large and of wood, as were the ones Brendan used for his longer voyages. In this maritime environment, Brendan grew up. He played with his companions, his brothers Domaingen, Faitleac and Faolan and his sister Briga and he learned the ways of the sea and of seafarers. He learned to make, repair and sail boats and he learned navigation and the rules of survival at sea that were to serve him well throughout his long life. He would have gone by sea to visit his mother's people in West Kerry.

The maritime tradition was very strong among the Alltraighe, indeed they were known as the *feara feorna*, people of the shore, people who grew up with the sea at the centre of their consciousness and culture. It was with this consciousness and in this culture that Brendan grew to manhood. The challenge and call of the sea was in his blood. He looked out from his home at the great Atlantic framed by Kerry Head and Brandon Point and he dreamed dreams of what lay beyond the horizon, dreams that he would make reality. He would have played on the beach called the Dock at the north-eastern end of Fenit Island and paddled across the mouth of Barrow harbour to Barrow. He looked to the east and, a league away, saw the *cathair* (city) of Áirde mac Fidaigh, his foster father, standing high above Listrim.

From the north of the island he looked at the bare rocks of Ilaunacusha, the Crow and the Rose. Further out were Muckalaghmore, Oileannabarnagh with its masses of seals, and the Báidin, further east, all inviting exploration on calm sunny days. Beyond them, Kerry Head and the home of Bishop Erc, Cillmhicadheadaigh. Further to the west, the Maharees and the Maharee Islands stood inviting. Rising above them, the mighty bulk of Sliabh Daidche that one day would be called Brandon by a proud people. To the south he saw the mile-long Fenit Island Strand running down to Little Samphire Rock with its gaggle of shags, standing tall, shaking out their wing feathers in the sunshine.

To the north-east lay the six-mile stretch of Banna Beach, running all the way to Ballyheigue, broken only by the Black Rock. Beyond Banna Beach lay Ardfert, and Tobar na Molt, where Brendan was baptized, and Tearmon Eirc, where Bishop Erc had his see. And then, on summer evenings, he watched the sun set, north of the Maharees, its long light shaking across the ocean swell, and, ever so rarely, as it disappeared beneath the rim of the sea, giving the green flash that is nature's gift to the dreamer. Where went the sun with its panoply of orange and green?

To understand Brendan is to understand this call of the sea. Many cannot understand this call of

The rough and rude Atlantic,
The thunderous the wide
Whose kiss is like a soldier's kiss
That cannot be denied.

Allied to Brendan's missionary zeal, this call of the sea meant that Brendan spent most of his 94 years in travelling, mainly by sea, founding monasteries in Ireland, Scotland, Wales and Brittany. One who knows the call of the sea knows why Brendan had to go; others will not understand.

One other factor that excited the mind of Brendan is an idea we also find in the writings of St Patrick. Both were influenced by the writings of Jerome (d. 420), Augustine (d. 430) and many others who believed, like the early Christians, that the last days were upon us as the gospel had now been preached to all the world, or soon would be. Writing on the psalms, Augustine says, "So it is that God's word has been preached not only on the continent, but even in the islands that are set in the middle of the sea; even they are full of Christians, full of the servants of God" and, writing to Hysicius, he says, "There are no lands, no Islands where the church is not." Jerome, writing against Pelagius, says, "Even Britain, the province fertile in the breeding of tyrants, and the Irish peoples, and all the barbarian nations round to the very ocean, have come to know Moses and the prophets." Both Patrick and Brendan wanted to be part of the final mission to peoples at the end of the earth. This is the clearest message in Patrick's *Declaratio.*

BRENDAN'S PREPARATION FOR HIS LIFE'S WORK

Brendan grew up under the watchful eye of Bishop Erc and, around eighteen years of age, felt that he had learned much already about the scriptures, Latin and, doubtless, the history of his own people. He wished to learn more and had heard about the saints of Connaught. So with the blessing of Erc, and a sharp warning about women from St Ita, he set off. In Galway he met Jarlath, the patron saint of Tuam and stayed with him some years. He was instrumental in helping Jarlath find the place where he set up his great monastery of Tuam. Then Brendan went further to the plain of An (Magh Enna, now Moyhenna, near Turlough, County Mayo, sometimes called Aí) which spans Roscommon and part of Mayo. It is around Cruachu, the seat of the kings of Connaught. Cruachu is, of course, famous as the seat of Maeve and Ailill who were responsible for the Táin Bó Culainge.

More important for us is that from this area came the Ui Neill of Ulster and Tara. Before migrating north to become the Cenél Conaill and the Cenél nEoghain, and east to become the southern Ui Neill, kings of Tara, they were a powerful element in the raiding parties that harried England, Scotland and Gaul. Their mythical ancestor was Conn of the hundred battles. Their more immediate ancestor was Niall of the nine hostages, who is reputed to have brought St Patrick to Ireland. Niall had several sons of whom three concern us here, Conall Crimthann from whom descended the Southern Ui Neill, Eoghan, from whom the Cenél nEoghain, and Conall Gulban, from whom the Cenél Conaill. It is quite likely that whoever captured Patrick in such a raid came from this area of Connaught or further to the north-east in the region of Sligo where the battle of Cul Dreimhne would later be fought. Hence Patrick spent his captivity near the wood of Foclut, to the west of Killala bay in County Mayo.

One may be allowed to speculate that many other hostages and exiles were to be found in this plain of An and there may well have been a tradition of ascetic monasticism here. In any case, it was here Brendan came to learn his rule. The books say that an angel dictated it to him; it seems more realistic to imagine that the angel had a human form and had a tradition from Ligugé and Marmoutier. Anyway, Brendan wrote down the rule which was still extant 200 years later, but of which we now have no trace. Brendan then returned to Erc and was ordained by him about the year 512. Bishop Erc died in 514.

Then began Brendan's life's work of travelling, teaching and founding monasteries. These foundations are to be found in many parts of Ireland, Scotland, Wales and Brittany.

BRENDAN'S APOSTOLIC WORK AND FOUNDATIONS

Brendan's apostolic life spanned some 65 years, years that were filled with activity, from 512 to 577. It is difficult to give a definitive time-scale for the various elements of that life. We may give a tentative breakdown thus:

- His initial foundations locally in Ireland
- His time with Finnian of Clonard
- His first voyage to the Scottish Isles, to the Faeroes, to Wales and to Brittany
- His foundations in other parts of Ireland – after 550
- His second voyage, in a wooden ship, in search of the Promised Land of the Saints
- His return to Clonfert and his death in 577

His initial foundations locally in Ireland

Many foundations in North and West Kerry claim Brendan as founder. In his own district, his great foundation was Ardfert, near the place of his baptism. Legend has it that the site of the foundation was dictated by a large bird who took the paper on which were written the plans of the monastery from the originally designated site, at Kilkeakle, some miles to the north and dropped it on the present site of Ardfert cathedral by the river Thyse a short distance to the east of Brendan's Well. Another local foundation was Kilmore at Kilfi-noora (Kilfenora, the Church of the Bright Gleam, Finabhair, an alias of Brendan), a mile or so to the east of Fenit. We find the same name west of Mount Brandon at Ballynavenoorah, the homestead of Finabhair. Near this latter foundation is another of Brendan's, Shankeel. Close by, but 3,000 feet above, is the oratory of Brendan on the very top of Mount Brandon. Further west we find an oratory associated with Brendan on Inistuascairt Island.

A disciple of Brendan's, St Beoanus (who is mentioned in one of the visions of St Fursey who took his relics with him to Britain and France), another relative and pupil of Brendan's, founded the "Laura" in the Glen below Ballinskellligs. Thither, often, Brendan came by naomhog to visit. Another relative and disciple of Brendan's was St Finan Cam, great-grandson of Airde Mac Fidaigh, Brendan's foster-father. He founded Inisfallen and Aghadoe in Killarney. Doubtless, Brendan often visited him who is credited as being the only one who could look directly at the face of Brendan (cf. the Irish Life in Part 2). Finan is called "Cam" because of a peculiarity in one of his eyes.

His time with Finnian of Clonard

Brendan, after his journey north to Jarlath and the Plain of An, maintained constant friendship with the other saints of Ireland. So we find him, probably about 540, going north to Clonard, the great school of St Finnian on the banks of the Boyne in County Meath. It did not bother Brendan that he was older than his master. Finnian had spent years in Wales with David and Cadoc, two of the triumvirate of great Welsh saints of the early sixth century. The third saint, who in turn would influence Brendan, was Gildas the wise. Gildas had taught in Armagh and had been rector there during a time when Wales was unsafe. He later returned to Llancarvan in Wales, wrote *The Destruction of Britain*, and founded a monastery in St Gildas de Rhuys in Brittany, where Abelard was to do penance some 700 years later. It may well have been Finnian who influenced Brendan to go to Wales.

Finnian of Clonard is known as "Tutor of the Saints of Ireland". With Brendan at Clonard were many of the great figures of Irish monasticism, and he seems to have made friends with all of them, friendship that would last all his long life. Such were Columcille, Brendan of Birr, Kieran of Clonmacnoise, Kieran of Saighir, Canice of Aghaboe and Kilkenny, a distant relative of Brendan's, and Ruadhan of Lorrha. What a mighty group they were! Of them all, Brendan seems to have been closest to Canice. We find the two travelling with Comgall of Bangor and Cormac of Durrow to see Colmcille in Eileach na Naoimh (Hinba) in the Garvillach Isles, some 25 miles east of Iona, where Colmcille had a retreat.

His first voyage to the Scottish Isles, to the Faeroes, to Wales and to Brittany

Brendan was known as the Navigator because he was the most intrepid and successful of the early Irish *peregrini pro Christo*. His reputation began with his basically inshore, or island-hopping, travels to Scotland, to the Scottish isles, including St Kilda, the Hebrides and the Orkneys, and to the Faeroes. Later he would go to Wales and to Brittany. He used the traditional large *naomhóg*, or currach, for these journeys and brought with him anything from twelve to twenty brothers.

We have seen that Adomnán called him "the greatest founder of monasteries of them all". David Camerarius, in 1631 in the Calendar he wrote for Charles I, King of England and Scotland, calls Brendan "the Apostle of the Orkneys and the Scottish Isles". Brendan was in Scotland 20 years before Colmcille and left his mark. In St Kilda, the farthest west of the Outer Hebrides we find Brendan's cell and the Hebridean fishermen, when in danger, used to call out "Branuilt, Branuilt" derived, according to George Little, from "Brenainn-a-shelodais", Brendan the Navigator. Brendansvik and Brandan's Bay in the Faeroes remind us of his presence.

Brendan's name is found in many parts of Scotland; to name a few, we find Dun Bhrenain on Hinba, a nearby island is Culbrandon. Brendan is associated with Tiree north-west of Iona; St Brendan's cross used to stand on Iona itself; in Barra is St Brendan's church, cemetery and road; to the North, above South Uist, is Kilvranan. We find Kilbrandane in Mull, Kilbrannan in Islay and Kilbrandan in the island of Seil. Near Oban is Kilbrandon. Near Banff on the North Sea we find a megalithic circle known locally as Brandan's Stanes. There are several St Brendan's havens. Kilbrennan Sound divides Arran from Kintyre.

The island of Bute is reckoned to be named after Brendan's hut, or Botha in Irish. The people of Bute were known as Brandanes, so the Martyrology of

Aberdeen tells us. And there are many more Scottish features which owe their name to Brendan. (Brendan surely never got to Argentina, yet south-west of Buenos Aires is the large expanse of the Bahia Samborombón – St Brendan's Bay – into which flows the Samborombón river.)

Next Brendan went to Wales. He must have known, in Tralee, Mór, the sister of David of Menevia, and he at least knew by reputation Cadoc and Gildas, both of whom had spent lengthy periods of time in Ireland. He spent time with them in Llancarvan and set up his own hermitage near Bristol in the Bristol Channel, Cadoc and Gildas also had hermitages there until Orkney pirates drove them out. Clearly Brendan wasn't wholly successful in his mission to the Orkneys!

Brendan seems to have spent considerable time in Wales. There Macutus came from Monmouth to be his student. Macutus was to spend many years with Brendan after he left Wales. He accompanied Brendan on his major voyage in search of the Promised Land of the Saints. He is better known as St Malo of Brittany who had his own monastery eventually at Aleth near the present town of St Malo. Brendan set up a foundation on the nearby Isle de Cezembre. Later hagiographers wrote a life of St Malo in which they stole Brendan's voyage story, sometimes with thinly disguised variations, giving Malo the principal role with Brendan as assistant, though Brendan is always referred to as "the master". Otherwise, the voyage of Malo is very much the same as the *Navigatio Sancti Brendani Abbatis*.

It was now approaching the middle of the century and Brendan had given nearly forty years to teaching, travelling for Christ, and founding monasteries and hermitages. He was around 65 years of age; it was time to return to his own people.

His foundations in other parts of Ireland – after 550

Brendan found things had changed in Fenit. For whatever reason, but most probably due to shifting population pressure and inter-family power struggle, Brendan's people, the Alltraighe, along with many of the Ciarraighe, had been evicted from, or otherwise left, their lands in Alltraighe-cuile and other parts of Kerry and gone up the Shannon to Galway, Roscommon and the Plain of An. Ciarraighe Uacthar (Upper Kerry) can be found here. They were led by Coirbri MacConuire. The Ciarraighe settled in large areas and became known as Ciarraighe-Aei, Ciarraighe Locha na n-Airneadh and the Ciarraighe Airtich.

The Connaught king who received them, Aedh Mac Eochaidh Tirmcarna, knowing a good thing when he saw it, married a Kerry woman, the daughter of Coirbri MacConuire. This union resulted in the Ciarraighe getting large tracts of land around the plain of An. This did not stop Aedh rackrenting the Ciarraighe, but that is another story! It can be found in *Leabhar na gCeart*. This may well be the motivation for Brendan's coming back to Connaught – to help his countrymen.

The killing of Aedh's son Cornan by the high king Diarmait Mac Cearbhail, though Cornan was under the protection and sanctuary of St Colmcille, occasioned the famous battle of Cuildreimhne. Aedh fought in that battle and the high king Diarmait was routed with great slaughter. This battle was to have consequences for Colmcille, as we shall see later.

Brendan followed his people north. Before we follow him to his own people, we must look at his foundations outside his own county, many of which took place around this time. The first of these was on an island in the Fergus river near where the Fergus meets the Shannon in County Clare. The island is called Inis-dá-Dromand and the remains of the foundation can still be seen. He also made foundations in Doora, County Clare, and in Kilfenora in the same county. He had foundations in other parts of Ireland also, in Cork, in Dublin, in Wexford and in Kilkenny, at Cluain Imaire, two miles south of Inistiogue, on the left bank of the Nore, some five miles from Brandon Hill, to the East.

One of Brendan's first acts on returning to Connaught was to found a monastery at Cluaintuaisceart in the County Roscommon where he put his brother Faitleac in charge. Then going south-west he founded Inisquin (Inis-meic-ichuind), on an island in Lough Corrib, some 800 metres off the eastern shore. Here St Fursey, son of Fintan, a relative of Brendan's, would receive his first instruction. Next he went 12 miles south and founded the convent of Annaghdown where he put his sister Brig in charge. Then, probably looking for some place to be alone, he went to south Galway, below and across the bay from the present Roundstone, where he founded Inishnee at the end of a long finger of land. Next, he went north to the west coast of Mayo and established a refuge for himself on an exposed, virtually inaccessible, rock, Inish Glora, two miles off the Mullet Peninsula.

Inish Glora is part of the folklore of Ireland as it is there the children of Lir are buried, Fionnuala, Aedh, Conn and Fiachra, their graves marked by two flags a little to the east of Brendan's oratory. Despite its small size and its inaccessibility, Inish Glora has the remains of St Brendan's oratory and two little churches, the Church of the Men and the Church of the Women.

The final act of Brendan in Connaught was his most significant. In 561, the very day of the battle of Cuildreimhne, on land assigned to him by the local prince, Aedh Guaire, Brendan founded the abbey and school of Clonfert. For the next seven hundred years, Clonfert would rank with Bangor, Clonard, Clonmacnoise and Lismore among the great schools of Ireland.

We may pause here to mention two incidents that shed light on Brendan's character. Because of his involvement in the battle of Cuildreimhne and the human carnage that resulted, at the instigation of High-king Diarmait, Colmcille was arraigned before the synod of Teltown, in 563. He was censured and it looked as if he was going to be excommunicated. Then into the room strode Brendan to defend his friend. He carried the day, his reputation his strength. Colmcille was acquitted and, shortly after, left Ireland for Iona and Scotland.

The other incident concerns Aedh Guaire who was one of Brendan's principal benefactors at Clonfert. Aedh killed the high-king's herald who had come to collect tribute, and he fled across the Shannon for sanctuary to Bishop Senach who transferred him, for safety, to St Ruadhan of Lorrha in Tipperary. Diarmait came and, once again, violated sanctuary and took Aedh back to Tara for trial and execution.

Ruadhan called on Senach and Brendan and the three proceeded to Tara with crozier, book and bell. They pleaded for leniency for Aedh Guaire. Diarmait would have none of it and executed Aedh. Whereupon the three clerics stood outside Tara with crozier and bell and cursed Tara, saying that never again would king or queen reign there. And so it happened. Next year, 565, Diarmait was killed and thenceforth no king or queen reigned in Tara. There is a lesson here about the times and the people who lived in them! Diarmait had been very well disposed toward Brendan and had richly endowed Clonmacnoise yet we have plenty evidence of arrogance on both sides.

His second voyage, in search of the Promised Land of the Saints

Brendan was now 80 years of age and the wanderlust came upon him again. This was intensified by the tale of Barrintus which will be found in the *Navigatio*. He went to Westport, County Mayo, where he built a wooden ship with iron fittings, built by artisans who accompanied him on his voyage. When it was finished, he embarked with 60 companions on 22 March. This date is given us in the Martyrology of Tallaght where a feast is commemorated, the *Egressio Familiae St Brendani*. This feast was being celebrated before Aengus Cele-De wrote the martyrology in 787.

The *Navigatio* can speak for itself. We may deal here with two questions. First, did Brendan get to America? And, secondly, what does the *Navigatio* mean? The answer to the first question is that it is very likely that he did. It goes beyond our remit, here, to examine the archaeological, literary, linguistic and genetic evidence that is being revised daily. If Brendan did not reach the promised land, some others did and lived to tell the tale. We have evidence from classical times that people had gone well beyond the "pillars of Hercules". The Norse sagas tell of finding evidence of Christian remains and practices before them in "Vinland", on the East coast of the United States before the end of the first millennium.

The fact that the voyage tales became associated with Brendan who may not have partaken in them himself, augments rather than diminishes his reputation as a navigator. Many of the sights listed in the *Navigatio* have been identified with the island fauna of the Faeroes, the volcanoes of Iceland, the icebergs of Greenland, the fog of Newfoundland and the flowers and grapes of Florida. Other places may be associated with Brendan's first voyage: Ilaun na Mil in the Maharees, spouting like a whale, Árdilaun off west Galway, St Kilda of the cliffs and many places in the Shetlands and Hebrides. Discussion about these places can be entertaining but rather fruitless.

What about the meaning of the *Navigatio?* To answer that question we must begin in Newgrange in the Boyne Valley. Newgrange is a magnificent construction, 5,000 years old. It is magnificent in its engineering, magnificent in its art and magnificent in its cultural significance. Newgrange was built long before the Celtic people came to Ireland. It was built by our ancestors, for the Irish are not predominantly Celtic but Neolithic Indo-European. Genetically, the people of England are more Celtic than the Irish are.

Since our first ancestors came to Ireland some 10,000 years ago there was no large-scale invasion or movement of people into Ireland until the seventeenth century. Certainly, some Celtic people came and their culture dominated that of the indigenous people. Linguists tell us that the vowels of the pre-Celts have made Irish unique among Celtic languages. The Celtic culture and mind-set was more akin to what went before it than it was to the classical culture of Greece and Rome. In the classification of Max Weber, it was a non-rational, expressive culture as against the rational efficient culture of the Roman empire.

Alongside Newgrange we may put the Book of Kells. This can claim to be the world's outstanding work of art, yet so different from the works of the classical culture. It well illustrates the exotic expressive mindset of the Irish people. The pages are full of extravagant animals and intertwining, sometimes endless, lines and figures. Of such stuff is the *Navigatio* created.

So when we look at Newgrange and later Celtic masterpieces, we understand that we are dealing with a people who solved engineering problems long before the pharaohs did, who had a deep understanding, or questioning, of death and other issues, and who had an intricate art system that is very different from classical realism and logic. The intricate whorls on the great stones of Newgrange and on the pages of the Book of Kells, speak of a culture and communication system that we can only vaguely guess at. Scholars have opined that the circular symbols, so common on the rocks of Newgrange and other megalithic monuments, represent the "close to death" and "out of body" experiences of some people who relate seeing a tunnel with light at the end, representing the passage from life to death to life again.

Arnold Van Gennep, in his 1909 book, *Les Rites de Passage*, claims that our understanding and ritualization of rites of passage involves three stages, separation (pre-liminal), transition (liminal) and incorporation (post-liminal). The tunnels and circles of Newgrange, the intricacies of the Book of Kells, represent these three phases as do our close-to-death experiences, as do our own minds, whether consciously or unconsciously. The incidents related in the *Navigatio* do exactly the same. First, we find the separation as Brendan sails into the unknown. Then one finds the transition, the narrow entrances, the canopies, magic fires crossing a chapel, streams of water with differing properties, the whale, all needing explanation by Brendan or by other holy man, usually a person in authority. Then, finally, the finding of the promised land after enduring opaque fog, and the return to Brendan's own homeland – a perfect circle!

A short time before the sixth century of our *Navigatio*, the old ways of thought and expression held strong. Suddenly, an entirely different mode of thought and expression was being imposed on minds that had not, themselves, changed greatly. One can read much that has been written about the results of the imposition of Christian theology and classical logic on a people who had never known the discipline of the Roman empire; very little thought is given to the struggle in the minds of those who were exposed, not to a new discipline, but to an entirely new mind-set.

How naively we understand the changes of the fifth and subsequent centuries in pedagogical terms, in the substitution of one surface system for another, one catechism for another. The challenge was not on the surface, it was much deeper, more elemental, more entrenched in Irish society, in Irish culture and in the Irish psyche. An effort to understand the mind of those who created Newgrange and the Book of Kells through the spectacles of modern theology, jurisprudence or science is doomed to failure. Worse than failure is the fact that we end up deluding ourselves that our failure is fact, that we have succeeded in understanding the mind of those who had 5,000 years of a very different set of cognitive and communicative categories.

Thus, so easily are documents like the *Navigatio* written off – because they do not fit one of the categories of modern understanding and so must be fanciful fiction.

The *Navigatio* is a very complex effort to explore the new doctrines of Christian faith and to reconcile them with the categories of thought that had been inherited over thousands of years. The *Navigatio* is a catechism for a radically changing society with a mindset that was trying to reconcile the old with the new. What may be missed is that when deeply-ingrained cultural categories of thought are upset, the whole human psyche is threatened; one faces a calamitous breakdown of self and society. How simple we make the change to Christianity; how little we appreciate the difficulties.

Basically, the *Navigatio* is an exploration in poetic, imaginative and artistic form of the fundamental questions of human life. For the moment, let us forget about Brendan. The important question is not the naive one of where did he get to? The important question is: What does the *Navigatio* mean? Anyone who reduces that question to geography or navigation, to "Where did he go?" is never going to have the least understanding of the *Navigatio* or of the visions of Fursey, of Tundal or of Owen. By the same token, neither will one understand Dante who, at a new crisis of civilization and culture, took so much from these Visions which, in turn, were based on the *Navigatio*. Nor, indeed, will one understand Michelangelo, Da Vinci or the other great interpreters of change.

The *Navigatio* explores and expresses an understanding of the relationships between the human being and God, the nature of good and evil, the relationship between justice and mercy. In the relationship between High-king Diarmait and people like Colmcille, Brendan, Ruadhan, Ciarán of Clonmacnoise and others like Cornan and Aedh Guaire, there is the canvas on which are written many of the great questions of the day, questions about power, privilege, generosity, justice and mercy.

The answers we find in the *Navigatio*, insofar as our modern minds can interpret them, may not be to our liking, but they are a genuine effort to understand the basic questions we have outlined above and to come to an answer, an answer that is not set out in the syllogistic logic of the Schools but in the representative expressionism of little Ethiopian devils and, above all, in the interaction with Judas and with the singing birds.

The birds are angels who did not support God during the rebellion of Lucifer, yet they were not guilty enough to be sent to hell, living now in a kind of pleasant Limbo. A small crack is appearing in our understanding of the aweful justice of Almighty God. Judas, the archetype of sinner and traitor, even Judas has some respite through the mercy of God tempering His justice. The doctrine of Purgatory is being developed in these scenes when they are applied to the ordinary human being.

What has gone before is but an effort to ask that we leave behind our modern scientific, analytic mentality and see the *Navigatio* for what it is, in its own way as challenging to interpretation as are Newgrange and the Book of Kells. I might ask the reader to remember my earlier comments on an Atlantic storm and what it can do to one's consciousness of reality. I have no doubt that some of the imagery of the *Navigatio* was developed during such storms or during long lonely watches where all the world seems to have disappeared except for the endless ocean water. I have spent three days, off the Newfoundland Banks, in fog so thick we could not see the prow of our 31-foot boat. Eventually, in such a situation, a feeling of unreality threatens one's consciousness; one is all alone; the rest of the world is no more.

Daniel De'Angeli, an Argentinian artist, has produced a series of 28 pictures on the voyage of Brendan. For those who would understand, this artistic, mystical and imaginative approach is the way forward. To quote from a letter of De'Angeli, "The ways of Saint Brendan are mysterious and powerful. The older I get, the more convinced I am that everything associated with him partakes of his daring vision."

Those who have experienced the call of the sea, of the "lonely sea and the sky", and know the treatment nature can dish out during a full-blown storm, or in the lonely, sleep-threatened watches of the night, those will know what I am talking about; I'm not sure about others. There is a well known phrase "there are no atheists in the trenches". There are no atheists in an Atlantic storm either!

Brendan's return to Clonfert and his death in 577

There is little more to tell. Whatever Brendan had experienced at sea and whatever meaning was locked in the stories of birds and whales and monasteries and hermits, he had lived experiences that had little to do with actual places or people as they were in themselves. It is these as experienced in deepest consciousness that are recorded. I have no doubt that Brendan reached the American continent, but that is not important. He returned from sea, a changed man, with ever deeper understanding of God and people.

He had left Clonfert, in the care of his friend and relative, Bishop Moennu, who had come with him from his monastery at Killeanny near Castlegregory and had helped him build Inisquin with their own hands. Moennu and the other brothers greeted the returned travellers with great joy.

Soon, Brendan was on his way again, visiting his many foundations in many parts of Ireland. We can imagine him travelling down the Shannon to Clare and to Kerry, to Valentia, to the Skellig and to the Glen. Then back to Ardfert and Corca Dhuibhne and then to Inishnee and to Inish Glora where he could be alone.

At the age of 93, Brendan knew that his time was near, so he took himself to Annaghdown, to his sister Brig. There he died, on 16 May 577, after giving strict instructions that he was to be buried in Clonfert. So, hidden in a common cart, the body of Brendan was transferred the three-day journey to Clonfert and there he was buried. He had also advised Brig to go back to her own country of Fenit where she would be buried.

Moennu died in 571 and was followed by a succession of Bishops. who acted, first as coadjutors of Brendan, and then as his successors. Brendan remained a priest all his life and, as was normal at the time, had subject to his jurisdiction a bishop who could perform the Episcopal sacramental functions for the community. After Moennu came successors, Fintan the Melodious, Senach the Rough and Colman the Guileless. Next came the greatest of all the abbots of Clonfert, Kerryman Cummian Fada, a man of deepest learning and one who was regarded as fit to fill the position of pope.

Clonfert maintained its reputation as one of the great schools of Ireland, attracting students from all over Europe until the coming of the Normans in 1169. It was suppressed by Henry VIII and passed into Protestant hands in 1571. Clonfert had survived many burnings and lootings at the hands of Vikings and native Irish, and finally fell to political greed.

SOME FINAL THOUGHTS

St Brendan of Fenit, Ardfert and Clonfert, has been sidetracked into a mythical figure sailing endless oceans, meeting Judas Iscariot, speaking with birds and landing on the back of a whale.

The real Brendan was a much more interesting person. As we have seen, he grew up in comfortable circumstances in a Christian community in Fenit and learned the ways of the sea and the making and handling of boats. He had imbibed some of the teachings of Augustine and Jerome who thought that the end of time was near as the Gospel had been preached to almost all the peoples of the world. So Brendan dreamed of bringing the gospel to the final few peoples who had not yet received it. He looked out west and north over the Atlantic and asked himself if there were people out there that he might reach with the Word of God.

So began his travels. First to Scotland, to the Orkneys, the Outer and the Inner Hebrides, to St Kilda, to Islay and Bute, to Wales and to Brittany. In all these places Brendan founded monasteries or hermitages. In the meantime he founded monasteries in many parts of Kerry, in Clare, Kilkenny, Mayo and Galway.

David Camerarius, in the Calendar he wrote for Charles I in 1631, calls Brendan "the Apostle of the Orkneys and the Scottish Isles". Brendan was in Scotland, spreading the Faith, 20 years before Colmcille, whose work there has denied recognition to the work of Brendan. Indeed, Adomnán, the biographer of Colmcille, writing in 697, calls Brendan "the greatest founder of monasteries of them all".

What of Brendan's trans-Atlantic excursions? There is no doubt that Irish mariners went where Brendan is credited as going. It is of little import whether Brendan himself went; he was known as such a great traveller through all his 93 years that he was named "The Navigator" and the stories of his and others' travels became associated with him. And his spirit, which is what is important, spread throughout the consciousness of the emerging medieval Europe, carried by the accounts in the *Navigatio Abbatis Brendani*, that were, in translation, the first readers and "best-sellers" of the emerging languages of Europe. It is interesting that people emerging out of barbarism and facing the challenge of a new language in which to express their thoughts and feelings, should have chosen the *Voyage* as their manual and handbook. Surely, the contents of the *Navigatio* spoke to them meaningfully in this time of transition!

Brendan's experiences and the accounts of preternatural happenings in his *Lives* and *Navigatio* inspired the visions of his pupil St Fursey, of Tundal and of Owen with his visions in St Patrick's Purgatory in Lough Derg. Dante's *Divine Comedy* owes much to all four persons, especially to the *Vision of Owen*.

"Saint Brendan's Isle" was a permanent feature on charts of the Atlantic until the eighteenth century, sometimes put west of Ireland, sometimes west of the Canaries. This "Isle of Brendan" first appears on maps in 1125 and remains until 1700. An alternate name, "Brasail" (or, Hy-Brasil), appears until 1865! Up until 1721, explorers like Don Gaspar Dominguez searched for St Brendan's Island.

It is well established that Columbus went to look for St Brendan's Isle when he discovered the West Indies. As a student of the University of Pavia, Columbus would have learned of Brendan's voyage from the manuscripts brought there, seven hundred years previously, by Dungal, student of Bangor and founder of the University of Pavia. On the eve of his great voyage in 1492 he wrote: "I am convinced that the terrestrial paradise is in the Island of Saint Brendan, which none can reach save by the Will of God." Brendan was a man, not only of his time, but his spirit has inspired countless generations of people until quite recently. Why has his memory almost faded in our time? The answer lies in the political intrigue that has marked so much of Irish history.

The history of the early Irish church is little known. Many of the widely held beliefs about this church, particularly in its earlier times, are not factual but propaganda to suit the vested interests of secular and ecclesiastical powers, often acting in consort with one another. Many of the saints that we venerate have suffered because of the propaganda machine of these vested interests.

A feature of Irish life in the fifth century that must not be forgotten is the complete absence of towns. The first proto-towns were the monasteries, and their phenomenal expansion owes as much to the success of this first beginning of urbanization as to the Christian spirit of the inhabitants. In a chaotic world, the monastery-town provided stability, employment, social services, protection and peace. The idea of sanctuary and the veil of superstition that hung over things religious were no hindrance. Many, often most, of the inhabitants of monasteries were lay persons though they tended to be called "monks".

Apart from Ciaran of Clonmacnoise – called always, one suspects derisively, the "son of the wright" – all the early saints of Ireland were high-born or well connected. Colmcille was first cousin to the high king of Ireland, Diarmait; Brendan was of high rank. It suited the kings and chieftains of Ireland to have monasteries in their territories. They were the flagship enterprises of their day. They inculcated, by word and example the virtues that made the local peasantry a profitable commodity for the overruler. The sixth and seventh centuries were marked by devastating famines and plagues and, while, sometimes, whole monasteries were wiped out, they yet provided one of the few lights on a dark canvas.

Another aspect of the relationship between prince and abbot is illustrated by the *Córus Béscnai*, a civil law of the early eighth century that gave legal standing to what already had the force of custom: the successor of the abbot was to be a relative of the founder (*fine érlama*). If a relative of the founder was not available, the abbot was to be a relative of the potentate who gave the site for the foundation. This is clearly illustrated in the case of Iona, but is true also in the case of all other foundations. So the secular and ecclesiastical powers worked hand in hand in a happy symbiotic relationship. In time, this led to terrible corruption as St Malachy, abbot of Bangor, found when he was appointed bishop of Armagh in 1129; St Bernard says that "he found he was sent, not to men but to wild beasts". This was the result of eight generations of hereditary succession to the see of Armagh where monetary consideration was all that counted.

"Saint Patrick was a gentleman, he came of dacent people": so began a song that was popular some time ago. Like Brendan, the real Patrick is unknown to the vast majority of our people. He was a gentleman of decent stock as we know from his own writings, his *Declaration* (or *Confession* as it is better known) and his *Letter against the Soldiers of Coroticus*. He was not the all-conquering figure in green chasuble and mitre, driving druids and snakes before him, easing his way triumphantly through Ireland, a guest of kings and chieftains. Patrick was much more than this because his was not a triumphal march through the palaces of the great.

The exciting thing about Patrick was that he was a very limited person who made up in integrity and determination what he lacked in education, judgement and ability. Rather than moving triumphantly through Ireland, he bribed his way through officials, using up his own inheritance to free Christian slaves and to buy his way through the power structure that was the clan system of Ireland. Like St Paul, he suffered imprisonment and abuse, yet kept going. Interestingly, Patrick makes no mention of Armagh in his writings.

St Patrick worked very much in north Connaught, because that is where he himself had been a slave, There is no evidence that he ever had a mandate to work in Ireland. He seems to have come in answer to a vision he had, and left his episcopal assignment in England, entirely on his own initiative, a move that was expressly forbidden by the councils and the canon law of the day. For leaving his post (he seems to have been away seven years at the time) he was arraigned before an ecclesiastical court in England. His Declaration is his answer to this court. He came to Ireland in 461 and died in 493.

Why, then, were we all taught that Patrick came to Ireland in 432 and died in 461?

Simply because another, Palladius, had been sent by Pope Celestine of Rome "to the Christians in Ireland" in 431 and seems to have worked main-ly in the Midlands. Palladius brought with him, from Auxerre in France, other bishops, including Secundinus, Auxilius and Isernius Their churches are to be found in Leinster, in Dunshaughlin (Domnach Sechnaill – Church of Secundinus), in Killashee (Cell Usailli – Church of Auxilius) and in Kilcullen – the Church attributed to Isernius. It was the strategy of the time to found churches overlooking royal residences and important pagan ceremonial sites; Dunshaughlin overlooks Tara, Kilashee looks on Naas while Kilcullen looks out on Dún Áilinne, seat of the kings of the Laigin (Leinster).

Whence, then, the school of Armagh? Given the sketchy nature of our sources, one can only speculate. During the fourth century, Nennius became the apostle of north-west Britain and southern Scotland. He was educated in Rome and spent time with St Martin of Tours, whom we have already men-tioned. He learned the principles of monasticism from Martin, who also lent him masons to build his monastery, as stone building was unknown in the area at the time. Around 395, Nennius built his monastery in Galloway, on

Whithorn Island, to the east of Burrow head. Because of its white stone construction, this became known as the Candida Casa, the White House. Nennius dedicated his monastery to St Martin.

The monastery was 45 miles from the Ards peninsula in County Down. Here, in Ards, close together, would be built three great monasteries, Mochae's Oendrum, on an island in Strangford Lough, Finian's Moville (*c.*540) and Comgall's Bangor (*c.*555). The earliest of these was Oendrum (or, Noendrum, with the article before it). It is not possible to date the foundation of Noendrum, but tradition links it and the Ards peninsula with Whithorn. With the withdrawal of Roman troops from Britain in 410, the Scots and Picts descended on Galloway and, doubtless, some of the monks fled across to the Ards Peninsula. Just as there was interaction with Wales and Cornwall, and movement of peoples in the south-east, so was there with Scotland in the northeast, probably to an even greater degree. Thus, Down had its quota of Christians and monks even before Palladius came. Downpatrick and Saul, places associated with Patrick, are just at the other end of Strangford Lough, to the south. It was quite natural for Palladius to set up Armagh monastery overlooking the great ceremonial site of Eamhain Macha, or Navan Fort, the legendary home of the Red Branch Knights. The first bishop and abbot of Armagh could well have been Benignus who later became subsumed into the Patrick legend. St Patrick would have known of Candida Casa and of the Christians in Down and Armagh and, no doubt, made contact with them. The rest is history, or, more properly, propaganda.

To suit the ambitions of the Northern Uí Néill kings of the seventh and subsequent centuries, history was rewritten. Muirchú and Tirechán composed lives of Patrick in the mid seventh century which were written into the Book of Armagh. This book was composed by Ferdomnach in 807 under Áed Oirdnide, Armagh Ui Néill high-king of Ireland. Also copied into the Book of Armagh, was Patrick's *Confession*, but we have to rely on continental sources for what Patrick really wrote as Ferdomnach bowdlerized the work, taking out anything that might be taken amiss in regard to Patrick or reflect negatively on him. For instance, the account of his confession of fault to a friend is removed.

Palladius was written out of history along with the other pre-Patrician saints of Ireland, Declan of Ardmore, Ailbe of Emly, Ibar of Wexford and Kieran of Cape Clear and Saigir — southerners all. Also downgraded were the great saints of Ireland, Comgall of Bangor, Finnian of Moville, Finnian of Clonard, Kieran of Clonmacnoise, Kevin, Finbarr, Carthach of Lismore and many others, including Brendan of Ardfert and Clonfert.

The only three saints to be given the limelight were the three patrons of the three septs of the Ui Neill, Patrick and Colmcille of the Northern Ui

Neill and Brigid of Kildare and of the Southern Ui Neill. This political imposition is still with us, stronger than ever, due to ignorance of history among people, many of whom should know better. It is instructive to look at the Roman Missal in use in all Irish churches. The only Irish saints listed in the missal are Brigid, Patrick, Colmcille, Columbanus and, a recent addition, Oliver Plunkett, Northerners all.

Among those who might be expected to know better are two of our recent popes, Paul VI and John Paul II, both of whom have quoted from the book of Armagh a saying they attributed to Patrick, that Patrick never uttered – "Ecclesia Scotorum, imo Romanorum, ut Christiani ita et Romani sitis" (O Church of the Irish, nay of the Romans, as you are Christians, be you also Romans). It suits Rome that its pope should partake of the general ignorance regarding Patrick.

By the seventh century, the only real political opposition to the Cenél nEoghain power in Armagh was that of their kinsmen, the Cenél Conaill of West Ulster and their scion, Colmcille, whose monasteries ranged from Iona through Derry and Durrow to Swords. Control of monasteries was very important as their holdings were one of the principal sources of wealth and revenue at the time.[1]

With the onslaught of the Vikings in 795, and the killing of 68 Iona monks in 806, Iona and the Cenél Conaill lost power which became more and more concentrated in Armagh and the Cenél nEoghain. Due to a controversy about the timing of Easter, Iona had also lost out because they held out for the old Irish way of computing Easter long after the rest of Ireland, including Armagh, had accepted the Roman way. Armagh, and, at first, Kildare, had hitched their wagons to Rome, a ploy that would pay off handsomely!

Armagh went on to emphasize its dedication to Rome by using Roman bureaucratic terminology like "Metropolitan" and "Archiepiscopal hierarchy", words and concepts that were utterly foreign to the Irish church structure, yet which gave Armagh the edge in claiming Patrician (Armagh) jurisdiction over all Ireland, just as the Ui Néill were claiming like jurisdiction in the secular world. Indeed the struggle for hegemony between the northern churches is marked by the proclamation, nationwide, of the *Cáin* (tax or law) *Adomnáin* in 697, the *Cáin Colmcille* in 778 (both showing the power of the *Cenél Conaill*) and the *Cáin Pátraic* in 783 when the "relics" of the apostles that Patrick had supposedly brought to Armagh were paraded throughout Ireland to enhance the claims of Armagh.

---

1 This had serious repercussions later. The Annals of Ulster record a battle between the monks of Clonmacnoise and Durrow in 764 in which 200 of the monks of Durrow were killed!

The final irony is that, some time after Áed Oirdnide died (819 or 817), a king of Cashel, Feidlimid Mac Crimthann, established himself as the first high king of all Ireland in 838. This man had a curious history, becoming abbot of Cork in 836 and "occupying the abbot's chair in Clonfert" in 838. He proceeded to cooperate with Artri, bishop of Armagh, in bringing the Cáin Pátraic to Munster and establishing it province-wide.

Feidlimid was prepared to back Armagh's claim to ecclesiastical primacy as long as it bolstered his own secular power. He was to be followed in this gambit by Brian Boru who had Maelsuthain of Inisfallen write in the Book of Armagh, in 1005, in his presence as "Imperator Scottorum" that all ecclesiastical tribute and stipends should go to Armagh. The entry reads:

> Saint Patrick, when going to heaven, ordained that all the fruits of his labour, as well of baptisms, as of causes and other alms, should be carried to the apostolic city, which in Irish is called Ardd-Macha. So I have found it in the libraries of the Scots. This I have written, that is, Calvus Perennis [Mael Suthain], in the sight of Brian, Emperor of the Scots, and what I have written he determined for all the Kings of Maceria (Cashel).

Like Feidlimid, Brian had enough on his hands fighting for secular power. He was quite happy to ally himself with the most powerful ecclesiastical dynasty and allow them preferential access to ecclesiastical taxes. In fact, Brian Boru also had his eye on ecclesiastical power as he made his brother, Marcán, Abbot of Killaloe, Terryglass and Inis Celtra. Other potentates were doing the same.

Feidlimid died peacefully, a rarity for kings in those days, and is reckoned among the saints of Ireland in the Martyrology of Tallaght with a feastday on August 28th!

Meanwhile, the great schools of Ireland continued to educate the youth of Europe and to send missionaries to the continent. Bangor, in the North, Clonard in the centre and the southern schools of Clonmacnoise, Lismore and Clonfert were the greatest of these. The last two of these were founded by Kerrymen, Carthach and Brendan. Because of the political pressures of the time, the founders of these great schools never got the recognition that was their due. It is not too late to speak up for them and especially for Brendan. We need not establish commissions of inquiry into political and ecclesiastical corruption in the fifth to the eleventh centuries – we have enough of them already! What we need is an appreciation of true greatness that can only come from being well-informed.

PART TWO

The documents

THE IRISH LIFE OF ST BRENDAN

Birth, baptism and early life of Brenainn

Beatus vir qui timet Dominum, in mandatis ejus volet nimis. Blessed and righteous and perfect is he in whom are the fear and dread of the mighty Lord and who desires mightily to fulfil God's commands and teachings, even as this declaration is uttered in the canon of the Old Law and the New Testament.

Now there was a multitude of the patriarchs and prophets and apostles and disciples of the Lord, to whom, in the Old Law and the New Testament, this declaration was uttered, that they are blessed, righteous, perfect, advanced, because of the desire and extreme longing which they have to fulfil the commands and the divine teaching, and because of the fear of the Lord perfectly in their hearts and in their minds, without considering aught else save this alone.

One of those of the New Testament, of that happy blessedness, he for whom there is a festival and commemoration on the occurrence of this season and time, the seventeenth of the calends of June, was Brenainn, son of Finnlug, of the race of Ciar, son of Fergus. The head of the belief and the great devotion of all the world was this holy Brenainn; like unto Abraham the faithful; a chief prophetic psalmist like David the son of Jesse; a distinguished sage like Solomon the son of David; a lawgiver like Moses son of Amram; a gifted interpreter like Hieronymus, the prophet; a marvelous man of intellect like Augustine; a great reader of chief congregations like Origen; a virgin was he like John, the Lord's bosom fosterling; an evangelist like Matthew; a teacher like Paul; a chief apostle of forgiveness like Peter, the high apostle; a head of hermits like John of the Baptism; a commentator like Gregory of Rome; a prudent guide over land and sea, like Noah son of Lamech. And as Noah raised up the ark over the wave-voice of the flood on high, so then will Brenainn raise up his monks and his households on high over the fire of doom, so that neither smoke, nor mist nor spark will reach them, through the powers and fair devotion of Brenainn, son of Finnlug.

In the time of Oengus, son of Natfraech, King of Munster, this holy Brenainn was born. Of Ciarrai Luachra was he, of Alltraige Cuile in particular. Finnlug, a man free and of good race, devout and faithful, was the father of that child. That couple, Finnlug and his wife [Cara], in life and in lawful wedlock, were under the rule of Bishop Eirc. Now Brenainn's mother saw a vision before Brenainn was born: she had the full of her bosom of pure gold, and her breasts shining like snow. After that vision had been related to Bishop Eirc, he said that she would give birth to a mighty progeny, which would be full of the grace of the Holy Spirit, even Brenainn.

A certain wealthy man dwelt in a residence some distance from Finnlug's house: Áirde son of Fidach was his name. Bec Mac Dé, a chief prophet of that time came to Áirde son of Fidach's house.

Áirde asked of Bec, "What thing is nearest us tonight?"

Said Bec, "Tonight, between you and the sea, your own worthy king will be born and there will be a multitude of kings and princes who will adore him, and whom he will take with him to heaven."

In that night of Brenainn's birth, 30 cows brought forth 30 calves at Áirde son of Fidach's. Early next morning Áirde arose and kept asking for the house in which the little child had been born; and he found Finnlug's house, and the babe therein, and he knelt eagerly in his presence and offered him the thirty cows with their calves. That was the first alms that Brenainn received. Then Áirde son of Fidach took the boy in his arms and said, "This boy will be my fosterling for ever and ever."

Now, on the night of Brenainn's birth, Bishop Eirc saw Alltraige-Cúile under one vast flame, the like of which he had never seen before, and the manifold presence of angels in snow-white garments all around the land. Bishop Eirc rose early next morning and came to Finnlug's house and took the boy in his arms and said to him, "O man of God, take me to yourself as your own monk, and, though a multitude be glad at your birth, my heart and soul are glad."

Then he knelt before him and wept greatly in token of gladness. Then he baptized him, and "Mobhi" was given him at first as a name by his parents, as the poet said:

Mobhi his name at first
Given by parents, fair his face
A youth hostful, seeking, slender,
He was a help to the men of Ireland.

Thereafter, a white rain [*broen finn*], that is a white mist, poured down and filled all Fenit. Thence was Broen-finn his name; *find* "white" was said of him because he was white in body and soul, as the poet said:

> Braonfind his name after that,
> In body and in soul
> From that shower he was named
> By Bishop Eirc his mentor.

Then three purple wethers leaped out of the well as the fees for baptizing Brenainn, as the poet said:

> Three purple wethers, pleasant the herd,
> Baptismal fees for child Brenainn,
> Sprang – fair was the compact –
> Out of the well, alone.

His family took him with them and he spent a year with them. Then Bishop Eirc took him to his own foster-mother, Ita, with whom Brenainn remained five years. And Ita, the nun, gave him exceeding love, for she used to see the angels ascending and descending above him and the grace of the Holy Spirit manifestly upon him and Brenainn always called joyfully to the nun whenever he saw her.

One day Ita asked him, "What causes you such joy my holy child?"

"You", said he, "you, whom I see speaking to me continually, and virgins without number like you, and they nursing me fondly from one to another."

Angels were there in the guise of virgins:

> Angels in the guise of virgins,
> Were fostering Brenainn
> From one hand to another
> Without hurt to the babe.

Life with Bishop Eirc

Then, at the end of five years, Brenainn constantly read his psalms with Bishop Eirc, and Ita missed him greatly. Now Bishop Eirc had no milch cow, for he used to take alms from no one except a little from monks. Now, one day, Brenainn was asking milk from his foster-father: "God is able to do that, my son", said Bishop Eirc.

After that a hind came every day from Sliabh Luachra with her fawn, and he milked her, and after her milking she used to go back to the mountains.

Then dwelt Brig with him; she was an own sister of his, and exceeding was his love for her, for he could see the service of angels over her and her foster-father's countenance shining with the radiance of a summer sun.

On a certain day Bishop Eirc went to preach the word of God, and Brenainn, who was then aged ten years, went with him in the chariot. Brenainn was left alone in the chariot after the bishop had gone to preach and he sat in the chariot singing his psalms alone. Then a fine, full-grown, flaxen-haired girl, of royal race, came to the chariot to him, looked on him and saw his beautiful bright face. Then she tried to jump into the chariot and play her game with him.

Then he said to her, "Go home, and blame whoever brought you here." and he took the reins of the chariot and began to flog her severely so that she was crying and bawling and ran to the place where her father and mother, the king and queen, were waiting. Then Bishop Eirc returned and began rebuking him severely for beating the innocent maiden.

"I will perform penance for it", said Brenainn, "and do you tell me what I shall perform."

"Go into this cave till morning", said Bishop Eirc, "and stay there alone till I come to you tomorrow."

Then Brenainn sat down in the cave and he began there his psalms and his hymns of praise to the Lord. Bishop Eirc watched near the cave, listening to Brenainn without his knowledge. Now the sound of Brenainn's voice singing his psalms was heard a thousand paces on every side. The sound of the voice of Colombcille was heard to the same distance when he chanted his psalms and his hymns.

> The sound of the voice of melodious Brenainn
> In the cave near Fenit
> A thousand paces on every side
> His high delightful voice was heard

Then the cleric beheld troops of angels up to heaven and down to earth around the cave until the morning. From that day forward no one save only Finan Cam could look at Brenainn's face because of the abundance of divine radiance, for Finan was himself full of the grace of the Holy Spirit. And that is what allowed him, rather than others, to look at Brenainn.

To look on Brenainn's face
No one in Ireland is able
Save Finan Cam, dear the champion,
He alone, because of the greatness of his grace

On a certain day Brenainn and Bishop Eirc were travelling on the road. A certain young man came on the road into their company. It happened that enemies, seven warriors, were near him, and great fear seized the youth and he said "Those yonder will slay me now."

Brenainn said, "Go on a little to the shadow of that pillar-stone there, and stretch yourself on its shadow."

The young man did as he was told. Brenainn raised his hands to God and prayed that the young man might be saved in the form of a pillar-stone. Then his enemies came to the pillar-stone and they cut its head off in his shape, and they wounded the pillar-stone in its side, left the stone beheaded, and carried the head with them in the shape of the head of their enemy. And still, as the wise say, that stone remains in the same place.

So there Brenainn made a stone of the man and a man of the stone.

"Repent you," said Bishop Eirc, "for the head of the stone is what you have and your enemy has gone whole from you."

Then they made fervent repentance under Bishop Eirc's rule then and forevermore.

Brenainn learns the Rules of the saints of Ireland

Now, after Brenainn had learnt the canon of the Old Law and the New Testament, he wished to write down and to learn the Rules of the saints of Ireland. So Bishop Eirc consented that he go and learn these rules, for Eirc knew that it was from God that Brenainn had that counsel. And Bishop Eirc said to him, "Come again to me when you have those rules that I may ordain you."

After Brenainn had gone to commune with his foster-mother Ita, she said the same to him, that is, to learn the Rules of the saints of Ireland and she also said to him: "Do not study with women nor with virgins, lest someone revile you. Go," she said, "and a famous warrior of noble race will meet you on the road."

After Brenainn had traveled some distance, Mac Lenin met him. Brenainn said to him, "Repent, for God is calling you and you shall be His dutiful child from now on."

Then did Colmán mac Lenin turn to the Lord and built a church at once.

After that, Brenainn visited the province of Connaught, drawn by the fame of a certain pious man who lived there, Iarlaithe [Jarlath] son of Lug, son of

Trén, son of Fiach, son of Mochta, son of Bresal, son of Siract, son of Fiacha Finn. And from him Brenainn learnt all the Rules of the Irish saints.

And Brenainn said to Iarlaithe, "In no way shall your resurrection be here."

"My holy son", said Iarlaithe, "why do you hide from us the divine graces of the Holy Spirit which are clearly in you, and the innumerable powers of the mighty Lord which are secretly in your spotless mind? You came to me to learn from me, but it is I shall be yours from now on; only take me into your service for evermore; but tell me now where will be the place of my resurrection?"

Then Brenainn said to him, "As you are an old man, let a new chariot be made for you and travel in it on your journey; and wherever the two shafts of the chariot break, there will be your resurrection and the resurrection of a multitude along with you."

So the old man entered the chariot and he had not gone far when the two shafts of the chariot broke. The name of the place is Tuaim-dá-Ghualann. Thereupon, the two made this poem between them as they looked at the burial-place some distance away while the ministering of the angels about it was quite visible to them. Brenainn spoke the first five stanzas and then Iarlaithe spoke after him:

Brenainn

Lofty the graveyard of the splendid angels
Bright its splendour before my eyes;
Hell's torments will not be endured
By those who sleep in its clay.

The archangel marked it round with crosses
And consecrated its sod of green;
It is not the abode of the hideous demon
That shall be shown to us therein.

It will be a noble church with numerous clergy,
In it great synods will be held;
It will be a refuge for great and lowly,
There will be place for multitudes.

Should your monks forsake your church
Theirs shall be a time of tribulation;
Evil the ruin they suffer here,
Dooming to hell hereafter.

Your brothers will come in future time,
Summoned to the judgement seat,
You will be their advocate
If they follow your guidance now.

Iarlaithe

As long as they live obedient to me,
And while the cross remains,
They will banish their enemies afar;
They will shine like the sun.

As long as they live obedient to me –
I speak the truth in my verse –
Their sons shall survive them,
They will suffer not pain hereafter.

Happy he who takes the cross
On the hill of evergreen yews.
He will not see hell after judgement,
Whoever shall lie in its clay.

Be not angry MacDuach,
Its full price will I give you,
Heaven and abundance of riches,
And my corner of heaven forever.

Triumph will kings and clerics of your seed
As long as they are obedient to me.
No one shall claim their hostages
Every obstacle will they overcome.

After leaving Iarlaithe, Brenainn made his way toward Magh Aí. An angel met him on the road and said to him; "Write down from me the words of devotion."

Thereupon Brenainn wrote down from the angel all the holy ecclesiastical rules and that rule still exists. While they were crossing the plain, they saw a bier and a dead man on it with his friends bewailing him.

"Put your trust in the Lord," said Brenainn, "and the man you have will live."

After Brenainn had prayed to God, the young man arose at once to life and his family took him away with great joy. After this all the people stared at Brenainn and took him to the king of Magh Aí. The king offered him land wherever he liked in that plain, but Brenainn did not accept it, as he did not wish to stay in that plain.

Ordination and vision of Brenainn

Now, after Brenainn had written the Rule of the angel and the Rules of the saints of Ireland with their usages and their piety, he returned to Bishop Eirc who ordained him.

There he heard in the gospel: "Everyone who has forsaken father or mother or sister or lands for my name's sake shall receive a hundredfold in the present and shall possess everlasting life".

After that, the love of the Lord grew greatly in his heart and he desired to leave his land and his country, his parents and his fatherland, and he urgently besought the Lord to give him a land secret, secure, delightful, separated from men. As he slept that night, he heard the voice of an angel from heaven who said to him, "Arise Brenainn, for God has given you what you sought, the Land of Promise."

Then Brenainn arose, his mind glad at that answer, and went to a mountain at night and saw the mighty boundless ocean on every side, and then he beheld the beautiful noble island with trains of angels rising from it. He remained there for three days and again he fell asleep.

Then the angel of the Lord came to commune with him and said, "From now on and forever I will be with you and I will teach you to find the beautiful island which you have seen and which you desire to obtain."

Brenainn then wept copiously because of his delight at the angel's answer, and he gave fervent thanks to God. Thereafter Brenainn left the mountain and returned to his community of monks and said to them, "Build you three large vessels with three banks of oars in each ship and three sails of hides and thirty men in each ship."

But they were not all clerics, as the poet said:

Three ships the sage sailed
Over the foaming wave-voice of the ocean;
Thirty men in each vessel he had
On the storm-waves of the crested sea.

Three ranks of oars in each vessel,
Sweet music their rowing made,
Sails of hide ready to unfurl,
In the three ships he sails.

All were not clerics who went
On the voyage; sweet their mutual love;
The monks were humble, spare their mien,
Who sailed in the three vessels.

Brenainn's first voyage

Then Brenainn, son of Finnlug, sailed over the loud-voiced waves of the rough-crested sea, and over the billows of the green-crested waves, and over the abysses of the wonderful, aweful, relentless ocean, where they saw in its depths the furious red-mouthed monsters of the deep and many great sea-whales. And they found therein many beautiful, marvelous islands, wherein they tarried not.

Thus they abode for the space of five years on the ocean marvelous, strange, utterly incomprehensible to them. And during all that time they encountered no one and not one of all the crews suffered any want nor did body or soul of anyone suffer injury. And that was a wonder, indeed, for Brenainn had not allowed them to bring any provisions with them, saying that God would provide for them, wherever they might be, just as he had fed the five thousand with the five loaves and two fishes.

Now when Easter was near, the brethren were urging Brenainn to go on land to celebrate the Paschal feast there.

"God," said Brenainn, "is able to provide us with land in any place He pleases."

When Easter came, the great sea-whale raised up its huge bulk over the breakers and the noisy billows of the sea, so that it was level, firm land, like a green sward, equally smooth, equally high. And they went onto that land and there they celebrated the Pasch, spending one day and two nights there. After they returned to their ships, the whale at once plunged beneath the sea. In this way they celebrated Easter, to the end of seven years, on the back of the whale, as Cuimin of Conor says:

Brenainn loved lasting devotion,
According to synod and companions:
Seven years on the back of a whale;
Severe was this mode of devotion.

Because each year, as Easter was at hand, the whale would heave up its back, so that it was dry solid land.

On a certain day, as they traversed the marvelous ocean, they beheld the deep black currents of the rough-crested sea, and in them their vessels were in danger of foundering because of the vehemence of the storm. Then each of them would look upon the face of Brenainn, for exceeding great was the peril in which they were.

Brenainn raised his voice on high and cried out: "Enough for you, O mighty sea, that you should drown me alone, but suffer my companions to escape." Then the sea grew calm and the rushing of the whirlpools subsided at once. Thenceforth they harmed no one else.

The vision of hell

One day, as they were on the sea, the devil came in a form inveterate, awful, hideous, foul, hellish, and sat on the sail of the ship before Brenainn; and none of them saw him save Brenainn alone. Brenainn asked why he had come before his proper time, the time of the general resurrection.

"For this have I come," said the devil, "to seek my punishment in the deep closes of this black dark sea."

Brenainn asked him, "What is this; where is that infernal place?"

"Sad it is," replied the devil, "that no one can see it and remain alive afterwards."

However, the devil revealed the gate of hell to Brenainn. And Brenainn saw that rough hot prison, full of stench, full of flame, full of filth, full of the camps of the poisonous demons, full of wailing and screaming and hurt and sad cries and great lamentations, and moaning and hand smiting of the sinful folks; and a gloomy mournful life in cores of pain, in prisons of fire, in streams of eternal fire, in the cup of eternal sorrow and death, without limit, without end; in black dark swamps, in forts of heavy flame, in abundance of woe and death and torments and fetters and feeble wearying combats; with the awful shouting of the poisonous demons; in a night ever-dark, ever-cold, ever-stinking, ever-foul, ever-misty, ever-harsh, ever-long, ever-stifling, deadly, destructive, gloomy, fiery-haired, of the loathsome bottom of hell.

On sides of mountains of eternal fire, without rest, without stay, but hosts of demons dragging the sinners into prisons, wretched, heavy, strong, fiery, dark, deep, occult, empty, base, black, void, foul, stale, musty, ever-contentious, quarrelsome, wearying, deathful and lamentable; sharp, rough, windy, full of wailing, shrieking, lamentations and crying; keen, spectral. Worms curved, hard, valiant, big-headed and monsters yellow, white, great-mouthed; lions fierce, greedy; dragons red, black, brown, demoniac; tigers mighty, treacherous; scorpions blue; hawks red and tall; vultures red and sharp-beaked; stag-beetles black and hump-backed; flies sharp and beaked; leaches crooked, bone-mouthed; mallets heavy, iron; flails ancient, old-rough; sharp swords; red spears; black demons; stinking fires; streams of poison; cats scratching; hounds rending; dogs hunting; demons yelling; stinking lakes; great swamps; dark pits; deep glens; high mountains; hard crags; a hosting of demons; a filthy camp; punishment without ceasing; a greedy host; frequent fray; quarrel without ceasing; demons punishing; abundance of torture; a sorrowful life; a place wherein there are streams frozen, bitter, swift, of full fire; straits hard, craggy, sharp-headed, long, cold, deep, wind-swept, little, great; plains bare, flaming; hills pointed; glens hard, full of reptiles; bogs rough, thorny; woods dark, fiery; roads foul, monsterful; seas thickened surface-stinking; nails huge, iron; waters dark, bitter; places abundant, various; an assembly foul, ever-gloomy; winds bitter, wintry; snow frozen, ever-dropping; flakes red, fiery; faces base, darkened; demons swift, greedy; tortures vast, various.

Then his people asked of Brenainn: "With whom are you conversing?" say they.

Brenainn told them that it was the Devil was conversing with him, and he related to them a few of the torments which he had seen, as we have said, even as have been found in the old writings of the ancient law.

Then said one of his people to Brenainn, "Let me behold somewhat of those torments."

On being permitted to behold Hell with its many torments, he died forthwith, and this he said when dying: "Woe, woe, woe," said he, "to him who has come, and will come, into that prison!"

Thereafter then Brenainn made prayer, and that man of his people who died was brought again to life.

The sea maiden

It was not long after they had gone thence that they found the maiden smooth, full-grown, yellow-haired, whiter than snow or the foam of the wave; and she was dead, the blow of a spear having gone through her shoulder and passed between her two paps. Huge indeed was the size of that maiden, a hundred feet in her height, and nine feet between her two paps, and seven feet in the length of her middle finger.

Brenainn brought her to life at once, and then he baptized her and asked her concerning her kindred.

"Of the inhabitants of the sea am I," said she, "that is, of those who pray and expect their resurrection."

Brenainn asked her what she desired: "Do you wish to go at once to heaven, or do you wish to go to your fatherland?"

The girl answered in a language which no other save Brenainn understood, and this she said, "To heaven," said she, "for I hear the voices of the angels praising the mighty Lord."

So after the girl had partaken of the Body of Christ, and of His Blood, she died without any distress, and Brenainn buried her honourably there.

On a certain day when they were happily on the sea and they were rowing, they beheld a certain beautiful island and it was lofty. However, they found no easy harbour or port in it for entrance. They continued going round about it to the end of twelve days, and during that space they were unable to land on it. However, they heard men's voices therein praising the Lord, and they saw therein a church high, famous, delightful.

When they heard the sound of the voice of the folk of the island, Brenainn with his people straightway fell into their spiritual sleep. Now since they were not allowed to land on the island, from above a waxed tablet was cast down to them, and it was inscribed, and this was written on it:

> Spend no toil in trying to enter this island, for ye will never come into it; but the island which ye seek ye will find, and this is not it. And go to your country and to your land, for there is a multitude seeking you who would fain see you. And search the Holy Scriptures wherein has been said: "*Mansiones Dei multae sunt,*" – as if this were what was said: "The Lord has many places and other mansions apart form this island."

Then they turned from that island, and in token of the welcome and care of the folk of that island, they took with them the waxed tablet which it had given to them, and they used to read it every day as if it had been given them by God.

Now, on a certain day they were voyaging over the sea. An exceeding great thirst seized them, so that death was nigh unto them. Then they beheld the beautiful pure-brinked streams of water dropping and flowing out of the rock. The brethren asked, "Shall we drink the water?"

"Bless it first," said Brenainn, "in order to know what it is."

Now after blessing the water, and after singing hallelujah over it, suddenly the streams ebbed away, and then they beheld the Devil squirting the waters from him, and killing those that would drink them. So they were saved through Brenainn's powers, and their thirst disappeared straightway. Since then, that place is shut upon the Devil, so that from that time forward it did no ill to man or to other animals.

Return of Brenainn

Now after Brenainn had been for seven years a-voyaging, he turned again to his own country and land as he had been ordered at the island. Then came the folk of his country and his own tribe to meet him, and they were asking him how much he had from his voyage; and they brought him treasures and gifts as if they were giving them to God. Now after many of them had left the world, they then followed Christ; and Brenainn then performed many miracles and marvels, and healed the sick and freed the bound and expelled devils and vices.

Thereafter he communed with his foster-father Bishop Eirc. He then came to the place where his foster-mother Íta dwelt, and he asked her what he should do as regards voyaging. Íta made him welcome as she would have made welcome to Christ with His apostles, and this she said to him, "My dear son, why did you go on a voyage without taking counsel with me? For the land which you are seeking from God, you will never find it in those dead stained skins, for it is a holy consecrated land, and men's blood has never been spilt therein. However," she said, "build you wooden vessels, and it is thus you will most likely find the land in due time."

Brenainn's second voyage

So, after that, Brenainn went into the province of Connaught. And there he built a great marvelous ship and it was distinguished and huge. And he embarked in her with his household and people and they carried with them various plants and seeds; and then they took wrights and smiths who had entreated Brenainn to let them go along with him. Then came the buffoon to Brenainn and prostrated himself before him and said: "O Brenainn, take me for God's sake and have pity on my misery so that I may go with you."

Brenainn then assented and he entered the ship with them. Sixty men was their number, and they were all praising the Lord, and their minds were towards God as the writings declare. The direction they first took was towards Aran, to the place where Enda dwelt, and Pupu and Rochath; and they remained a month in their company. Then, after they had sailed westward from Aran for some time, they saw an island great, lofty, remarkable, beautiful. Therein were mice like sea-cats that filled the strand at once to swallow them up.

The brethren asked Brenainn "What do these mice want?"

"To eat us and swallow us up," said Brenainn.

Then Brenainn said to the buffoon "Go and partake of Christ's Body and Blood and go then to eternal life, for I hear the choir-singing of angels calling you to them."

That seemed good to the buffoon and he said, "Lord, what good thing have I done, since I am taken at once to heaven?"

So, after the buffoon had received Christ's Body and Blood, he leaped ashore at once with great joy and the sea-cats devoured him, all save for a few of his bones. And he was buried by the brethren, and his name is written in a martyrology, for he was a wonderful martyr. It is clearly from the mercy of the Lord that the notoriously sinful man who came last into the ship, should be chosen to go first into heaven. Even so shall every well-meaning person who shall come last into the church go first into heaven, through his excess of goodwill beyond those who had been before him: as Christ says, "The first shall be last and the last first."

Now, after they had left that island, a sudden illness seized the smith, so that he was near death. Brenainn said to him "Why do you marvel? Go to the heavenly kingdom as you have sought till today, or, if you wish to live still in the world, I will pray to God for you and you will find health." However, the smith said, "I hear the voice of the Lord calling me," and after partaking of Christ's body and blood, he went to heaven.

So there was a great question among the brethren as to the body being without burial, for there was no land near them. Then Brenainn said that the body should be buried among the waves of the sea, for he who made heaven and earth and the rest of the elements was able to constrain the waves of the sea to keep the body in them immovably. So, without reaching the land, they buried the smith among the waves of the sea, down, without rising to the top of the brine, without moving hither or thither, but as it were on land; and he will abide there without corrupting till the Day of Judgment comes.

After they left that place, they beheld a little insignificant land. After they had taken harbour there, the harbour was filled with devils in the shape of dwarfs and pygmies, with their faces as black as coal. Then Brenainn said "Cast out the anchor, for no one will be able to enter this country save he who shall fight human battles against devils and shall spill blood over them." So they remained there for seven days and nights, and then they could not raise their anchor from below, and they left it stuck among the rocks and left.

Now they were in great distress from the want of the anchor and the death of the smith, for they had neither an anchor nor a smith who could make one for them. Then Brenainn said to a priest of his household, "Do you the smith's work to the end of the month." So Brenainn blessed the priest's hands, for he had not learned smithying. Then the priest made an anchor so excellent that its equal was never found before it, and will not be found after it.

Then they voyaged westward on the ocean for a space. They found a small, delightful, beautiful island and an abundance of excellent fish that had left the seashore and were in the enclosures and in the cashels of that lofty island. While they were going round about the island, they saw a stone church and a penitent, white-faced old man praying within. The old man was bloodless and fleshless with only a thin leather on those hard-bare bones.

Then the old man said, "Flee swiftly, Brenainn. There is a great sea-cat here like a young ox or a three-year-old horse, overgrown from feeding on the fish of this sea and this island. Avoid you him." They got at once into their ship and rowed rapidly over the ocean. Then they saw the monstrous sea-cat swimming after them. Bigger than a brazen cauldron was each of its eyes; a boars tusk had he, fuzzy hair upon him, and he had the maw of a leopard with the strength of a lion and the voracity of a hound. Then each of them began to pray to God because of the greatness of the fear that possessed them.

Then Brenainn said, "Almighty God, order the monster away from us that he may not devour us." Then a huge sea-whale arose between them and the monstrous sea-cat. Each of them began drowning the other, and battling savagely, till each of them drowned the other in the depths of the sea, and neither of the two was ever seen again. Then Brenainn and his people gave thanks to God and turned again to the place where the old man lived. And the old man made them welcome and wept in great joy. He welcomed Brenainn with a poem.

An Irish hermit welcomes Brenainn

"Of the men of Ireland am I," said the old man, "and we were twelve men when we went on our pilgrimage; and we brought the monstrous sea-cat with us as a little bird, and he was very dear to us, and after that he grew greatly and never did us any harm. And eleven men of them are dead, and I am here alone, entreating you to administer to me Christ's Body and Blood, that I may then go to heaven."

Then the old man revealed to them the land they were seeking, the Land of Promise. So, after the old man had partaken of Christ's Body and Blood, he went to heaven. They buried him there in the island alongside his brethren, with honour and great reverence, and with psalms and hymns, in the name of the Father, and the Son and the Holy Spirit.

They reach the Land of Promise

After that they reached the land they had been seeking for seven years, the
Land of Promise; as the proverb has it, "*Qui quaerit invenit.*" When they had
come near that land, and wished to take harbour there, they heard the voice of
an old man who said: "You hardworking men, you holy pilgrims, you folk that
entreat the heavenly rewards, O ever-weary life expecting this land, stay and
rest a little from your labour!"

After they had been silent for some time, the old man said to them: "Dear
brothers in Christ, why do you not take this noble, beautiful land wherein a
human being's blood has never been spilt, and wherein it is improper to bury
sinners or evil men? So leave in your vessel everything you have, except a little raiment round you and come up."

After they had landed, each of them kissed the other, and the old man
wept exceedingly with the greatness of his joy.

"Search you and see," he said, "the plains of Paradise, and the delightful
fields of the land, radiant, famous, loveable, profitable, lofty, noble, beautiful,
delightful; a land odorous, flower-smooth, blessed; a land many-melodied,
musical, shouting for joy, unmournful; a place wherein you shall find health
without sickness, delight without quarrelling, union without strangling,
princedom without dissolution, rest without idleness, freedom without
labour, luminous unity of angels, delights of paradise, service of angels, feast-
ing without extinction, avoidance of pain, faces of the righteous, partaking of
the Great Easter. A life blessed, just, protected, great, loveable, noble, restful,
radiant, without gloom, without darkness, without sin, without weakness, in
shining, incorruptible bodies, in stations of angels, on plains of the Land of
Promise. Vast is the light and the fruitfulness of that island, its rest, its loveable-
ness, its dearness, its stability, its security, its preciousness, its smoothness, its
radiance, its purity, its lovesomeness, its whiteness, its melodiousness, its holi-
ness, its bright purity, its nobleness, its restfulness, its beauty, its gentleness, its
height, its brightness, its venerableness, its full peace, its full unity! Happy he
who shall be with well-deservedness and with good deeds, and whom Brenainn son of Finlug shall call into union with him on that side, to inhabit for
ever and ever the island on which we stand!"

Now that they had seen that paradise among the waves of the sea, they mar-
veled and wondered greatly at the miracles of God and His power, and they
greatly honoured and glorified the Lord after seeing those mighty miracles.

Now, thus was that old man, without any human raiment, but all his body
was full of bright white feathers like a dove or a sea-mew and his speech was
almost that of an angel. After he struck his bell, they recited terce. They sang

thanks to God with their minds fixed on Him. They dared not ask anything and they received their spiritual instruction of Him at the uplifting of the gospel.

This then was the preaching that Peter and Paul and the other holy apostles most often used to make, this preaching of the punishments and of the rewards, for they were displayed to them in the same way. This, then, is the preaching that Sylvester, abbot of Rome, made to Constantine, son of Helena, to the over-king of the world, in the great assembly when Constantine offered Rome to Peter and to Paul. This is the preaching that Fabian, Peter's successor, made to Philip, son of Gordian, king of the Romans, when he believed in the Lord and when many thousand others believed there; and he was the first king of the Romans who believed in the Lord Jesus Christ.

This, then, is the preaching which Elijah is wont to make to the souls of the righteous under the Tree of Life in Paradise. Now when Elijah opens the book for the preaching, then come the souls of the righteous in shapes of bright white birds to him from every point. Then he first declares to them the rewards of the righteous, the happiness and delights of the kingdom of heaven, and at that time they are exceedingly rejoiced. Then he declares to them the pains and punishments of hell and the banes of Doomsday. Manifest exceedingly is a countenance of sorrow upon themselves then, on Elijah and on Enoch, wherefore they are called the two Sorrows of Heaven's Kingdom. Then Elijah shuts his preaching-book. The birds then make an exceeding great wailing, and beat their wings against their bodies till streams of blood come out of them for dread of the pains of hell and of Doomsday.

Now since it is the souls of the saints, whose lot it is to inhabit forever the kingdom of heaven, that make that lamentation, it were meet for the men of the world, though they should shed tears of blood expecting Doomsday, *in quo die mala erunt*. Now there will be many evils and tribulations on that day, that is, on the Day of Judgement, *in quo die Judex justus sua suis reddet: impiis poenas, praemia justis*. Then will the Lord pay to every human being in the world his own wage. Punishment he has for the sinful, reward for the righteous. Then the sinful will be cast into the depth of the eternal pain, and the lock of God's word will shut them up under hatred of the Judge of Doom. Then the saints and the righteous, the folk of charity and of mercy, will be carried to the right hand of God the Father, to inhabit the kingdom of heaven forever. Then they will abide in that great glory, in the unity of the Godhead and the manhood of the Son of God, in the unity that is nobler than any unity, the unity of the holy, noble, almighty Trinity, Father, Son and Holy Spirit.

I beseech the high almighty God, through St Brenainn's intercession, may we all deserve that unity, may we reach it, may we dwell therein for ever and ever!

EXCERPTS FROM THE LATIN LIFE OF ST BRENDAN

Brendan founds many monasteries

When St Brendan had been ordained a priest by St Erc, he then received the holy habit of a monk; and many persons, forsaking the world, came to him from different directions to be admitted by him to the monastic life. He founded oratories and monastic houses in his native district, though not many at that period. But when he returned from his voyage in search of the Land of Promise of the saints, his religious foundations were widely extended through many parts of Ireland.

It was then that many persons brought large offerings to St Brendan, in the name of Christ; and many others, relinquishing their worldly possessions, were received into the religious life by the man of God, who founded divers oratories and monasteries in many parts of Ireland, in which, so the elders relate, three thousand monks were under his rule. And he made his own father a monk and his mother a consecrated widow.

Meanwhile, the saint had visited his foster-mother St Ita, who welcomed him tenderly, with an affectionate embrace, and who received great mental stimulation from the recital of the marvelous things he had seen on the ocean. Soon after, Brendan took his leave of her, with mutual benedictions.

He proceeded to a place called Inis-da-dromand, which lies in a northern estuary of the lower Shannon between Corcabaiscin and Kerry; and there he founded a famous monastery, where, within a brief period, seven members of the community died in the odour of sanctity, about whose sacred relics the mortuary chapel of that place was erected.

About the same time the saint blessed fifty rivers in various districts which had been without fish; thereafter, they abounded in fish. In the course of time Brendan passed into the district of Connaught, where land was granted him, on which he founded the famous city of Clonfert, in which he was buried.

St Brendan visits Scotland, Wales and Brittany

Soon after St Brendan set sail on his pilgrimage to Britain, and went to visit the most holy elder, Gildas, a very wise man who dwelt there, the fame of whose sanctity was very great. Before the saint arrived at the monastery, St Gildas told his monks to prepare a repast for certain zealous labourers in the Lord's vineyard who would be their guests on that day, assuring them that they would then see a second St Peter the Apostle, again in the flesh in the person of this father, who was a tireless worker for the Lord, but whose virtue and power with God he wished to put to some trial, in order that the fault on account of which he came hither had been already pardoned by God. Then he directed the door porter to secure the outer door with iron bolts until it was opened by divine power [...]

It was during winter, in the third year of his pilgrimage, that St Brendan arrived at the monastery, and snow had fallen copiously so as to cover the ground, but none of it fell on St Brendan or his disciples while they waited before the barred door.

The door porter noticed this from inside and called out to them, "Come in at once, and let your own merits open the door to you." Whereupon St Brendan directed his disciple Talmach to open the door for them, in the name of Christ; and when he, in obedience, put out his hand towards the door, the bolts at once drew back, and were no longer visible. They then entered and went toward the church of the monastery, the doors of which were closed against them in like manner.

But, St Brendan knowing that this was done as a trial of his virtue, only placed his hand on the folding door and said, "O church of Christ, my true mother, open to me." Instantly the seals or locks were broken, and the church lay open before them, when they went at once into the choir. Here St Gildas had a missal written in Greek characters, and this was placed on the altar for use at mass.

Then the sacristan said to St Brendan, by order of St Gildas, "Man of God, our father abbot commands you to offer the holy sacrifice; here is the altar prepared, and a missal in Greek letters, from which you are to read the mass as our abbot does."

When St Brendan opened the missal he prayed, "Grant unto me, O Lord Jesus. a knowledge of those unknown letters, as You have by Your power opened these doors that were barred against us." Truly all things are possible to the true believer, for St Brendan knew at once those Greek characters as well as he did the Latin ones he had learned from his infancy.

He then proceeded to say Mass and St Gildas himself and all his monks came to the church to receive Holy Communion from his hands [...] and made fervent thanksgiving. St Brendan remained at the monastery three days and nights.

After this the venerable St Gildas said to St Brendan, "Accept me now, father, as a disciple of yours and become the patron of this city and people."

But St Brendan replied "Here I must not tarry, for my resurrection shall be in Ireland."

Then St Brendan, having received the blessing of St Gildas and all his monks, as well as those of the inhabitants of the city, and having bestowed his blessing on them in return, took his departure from the place, and in another district of Brittany he founded soon after a monastery, named Ailech. In another place, in Britain in the district of *Heth*, he established a church, and a town around it, and there the holy father performed great miracles. Subsequently he sailed back to Ireland [...]

Brendan returns to Ireland and founds Inisquin

St Brendan then came to the country of Connaught, and went into an island called in Irish *Inis-meicIchuind* [Inisquin], where horses of the king were on pasture. Here the saint, when building an oratory, set the king's horses to draw materials. The holy bishop Moenu was there with St Brendan at the time.

When the king, Aedh son of Eathach Tirmcarna, heard of this, he declared in his wrath that he would surely put to death the person who had done him so great a wrong. In his rage he hastened to the island, but as he prepared to cross over in a boat, a violent storm suddenly arose, which agitated the waters of the lake from its depths for the space of three days, during which the king had to await a calm.

On the night of the third day the Lord appeared to him in a dream and said to him, "Take care you do no harm to My servant Brendan; otherwise you will soon meet your death." When the storm subsided, the king made a gift of the island, together with the horses, to St Brendan, forever [...]

Brendan founds Clonfert abbey

St Brendan was 77 years old when he founded his monastery and city of Clonfert; and while he tarried there, a certain monk who had come away with the saint from his parents in Britain, died in the monastery. On the third day after his death, St Brendan said to the holy Bishop Moenniu, "Place my staff on the body of the deceased brother." When the bishop had laid the staff on the body, already for three days cold in death, the deceased brother at once arose from the dead, and being restored to perfect health, was sent back, much strengthened in faith, to his own country of Britain [...]

Brendan visits the saints of Meath and the high-king

Once upon a time, St Brendan went to visit the saints who dwelt in the territory of Meath. At that time Diarmait MacCearbhail, who then reigned at Tara as monarch of Ireland, had a vision in a dream, in which he saw two angels taking the royal collar of gold from his neck and giving it to a man he did not know.

On the following day, St Brendan came to visit the king, who, when he saw the saint, told his courtiers that this was the man to whom he saw his royal collar given in his vision. Whereupon his wise men declared to the king that his vision meant that hitherto sovereign rule in Ireland belonged to the kings thereof, but that henceforward it should be shared with the saints of Ireland, and that the saint now present, Brendan, should have extensive jurisdiction throughout the land.

When St Brendan heard of this vision, and its interpretation by the wise men, he said that thus it would come to pass that all good things will be given in this life, as well as in the life to come, to those who truly serve God, according to the text "Seek first the kingdom of God, and his justice, and all other things shall be added unto you" (St Matthew 6:33). And King Diarmait rendered great honour to St Brendan, for he was a righteous and Christian king.

Brendan tells of the pains of hell

One day Brendan was on a journey and a great storm of hail and snow fell on him and his companions. Some of the brothers said to Brendan, "Holy father, the cold in the infernal regions is not more intense than what we feel now."

"You speak like ignorant rustics," rejoined the saint. "We have seen Judas, the betrayer of our Lord, in a dreadful sea, on the Lord's day, wailing and lamenting, seated on a rugged and slimy rock, which was now submerged by the waves and again emerged from them somewhat. Against the rock there rushed a fiery wave from the east, and a wave of icy coldness from the west alternately, which drenched Judas in a frightful manner; and yet this grievous punishment seemed to him a relief from pain, for thus the mercy of God granted this place to him on the Sundays as some ease amidst his torments. What, therefore, must be the torments suffered in hell itself?"

When the brothers heard this, they besought the Almighty god to take pity on their manifold miseries.

Brendan tells the brothers to trust in the Lord

One day, when Brendan was traveling through a forest, a violent storm raged, and, by the force of the gale, trees were blown down on every side as Brendan and his companions journeyed on.

One of the brothers said to the others, "We are in great danger from those falling trees."

Then Brendan told them, "One night, when all our crew were asleep in the boat on the wide ocean, I alone remained awake and we came to an island which had many openings through it. It was supported on four great legs over the sea, and between those legs our boat passed under the island, and so we sailed right through while the island stood above us. Know then, brothers, that God, who sustains that island over the sea in that manner, and who allowed us to sail safely under it, can save us without hurt from the danger of those falling trees."

On hearing this example, the brothers grew strong in their confidence in Christ.

Brendan prepares for death

The blessed soldier of Christ, Brendan, came to visit his own sister, Bryg, who, under his direction, was governing a convent of nuns at Eanach-duin [Annaghdown], in the province of Connaught and in the district of the Hy-Bruin.

Among other things, he foretold to her the place of her resurrection in these words: "Not here, but in your own country of the Tragei [the *feara forna*, or shore dwellers, of Fenit] will your resurrection be. Proceed thither, therefore, for the people there will obtain God's mercy through you; there you will find a house of monks, not of nuns; but God is now calling me to Himself, out of the prison of this body."

Whereupon, his sister, in great grief, said to him, "Beloved father, your death shall be the death of us all, for if in your absence during life, it was hard to live without you, what must it be when you are dead?"

Then Brendan said to her, "On the third day from this, I will go the way of my fathers."

While he was biding there, on a Sunday after he had offered the Holy Sacrifice of the Body and Blood of Christ, the venerable saint said to his sister and to the brothers who were with him: "My very dear friends, on this day the Lord my God summons me to life eternal, and, I charge you, in the name of Christ, to do exactly what I tell you if you would have my blessing. Conceal my death here until my body has been carried to my city of Clonfert, for there I have chosen the place of my resurrection. If the people hereabout come to know of my death among them, they will surely bury me here against my wishes. You will therefore act in this manner:

"Place my corpse in a waggon and cover it over carefully with other things. You will send only one brother in charge of the waggon, who will tell all who ask him that he is carrying the goods of the abbot Brendan to his own city of Clonfert. All who may meet him will then let him pass, except one man, a soldier named Curryn, blind of the left eye. This man will not believe the words of the brother but, more cunning than the others, will sharply question him as to what he was carrying so secretly, and will closely search the waggon. When he finds and recognizes my body, he will, in a terrible voice, order the brother to leave among them the saint of God. And addressing me, he will cry out : 'Here in our country you will be buried with all honour, so that your resurrection may be among us, O man of God.'

"Then the brother shall look into a trench beside him, and seeing a lump of pure gold, shall offer it to this soldier saying , 'Take this gold given by God, and let me freely go my way.' This the man will refuse and then the brother shall promise: 'You will have the chief power in your tribe, and your descendants after you, if you allow me to pass on.'

"But the man, not trusting this promise, will still prevent a passage; and then the brother shall declare to him, 'You will not have eternal life unless you permit the saint of God to be borne to that place where he ordered his burial; and a sure sign I give you of the truth of what I say, when I tell you the thought of your heart when you met me was to usurp the chieftaincy of your tribe by murdering members of your own family.'

"When the man will thus learn from another the secret thoughts of his heart, and will know thereby that what was promised would surely come to pass, he will allow the brother to proceed in peace with my body. The brother will thereupon earnestly bless him and go on his way rejoicing."

When his sister and the brothers heard this adjuration, and this prediction of what was to happen, they promised the holy father that they would do what he had commanded.

Death of St Brendan

Soon after this, St Brendan gave his blessing to his sister and to the brethren, and, proceeding to the convent, passed beyond the threshold. Here, raising his eyes to heaven, he said: "Into your hands, O Lord, I commend my soul; save me O Lord my God."

And then the aged most holy Brendan gave forth his soul to God, on Sunday, the 17th of the Kalends of June [16 May] having completed the 93rd year of his age. His corpse was afterwards placed in a waggon, and one brother was sent in charge of it, as the saint had directed, and everything occurred on the journey as he had foretold before he died.

A great multitude of holy men assembled from all quarters on the occasion, and his blessed body that had been borne, in the manner related, from the convent of Eanach-duin to his own city of Clonfert, a three days' journey, was buried in the place of honour, with all glory and reverence, with psalmody and spiritual canticles; Our Lord Jesus Christ reigning over heaven and earth, and all creatures, in union with the Father and Holy Spirit, for ever and ever. Amen.

Here ends the life of St Brendan, abbot and confessor.

THE VOYAGE OF ST BRENDAN

St Brendan hears about the Land of Promise

St Brendan, son of Finnlug Ua Alta, of the race of Eoghan, was born in the marshy district of Munster. He was famed for his great abstinence and his many virtues, and was the patriarch of nearly 3,000 monks.

While he was in his spiritual warfare, at a place called Ardfert-Brendan, there came to him one evening, a certain father named Barinthus, of the race of King Nial, who, when questioned deeply by St Brendan, could only weep, and cast himself prostrate, and continue the longer in prayer; but Brendan raised him up and embraced him, saying, "Father, why should we be thus grieved on the occasion of your visit? Have you not come to give us comfort? You ought, indeed, make better cheer for the brothers. In God's name, make known to us the divine secrets, and refresh our souls by recounting to us the various wonders you have seen upon the great ocean."

Then Barinthus, in reply, proceeded to tell of a certain island:

> My dear child, Mernoc, the guardian of the poor of Christ, had fled away from me to become a solitary, and found, near the Stone mountain, an island full of delights. After some time I learned that he had many monks there is his charge, and that God had worked many marvels through him. I, therefore, went to visit him, and when I had approached within three days' journey, he, with some of the brothers, came out to meet me, for God had revealed my coming to him. As we sailed to the island, the brothers came out of their cells towards us, like a swarm of bees, for they dwelt apart from each other, though their intercourse was of one accord, well grounded in faith, hope, and charity; one refectory; one church for all, in which to discharge the divine offices. No food was served but fruits and nuts, roots and vegetables of other kinds. The brothers, after compline, passed the night in their respective cells until the cock crew, or the bell tolled for prayer.
>
> When my dear son and I had traversed the island, he led me to the western shore, where there was a small boat, and he then said: "Father,

enter this boat, and we will sail on to the west, towards the island called the Land of Promise of the Saints, which God will grant to those who succeed us in the latter days."

When we entered the boat and set sail, clouds overshadowed us on every side, so dense that we could scarcely see the prow or the stern of the boat. After an hour or so, a great light shone around us and land appeared, spacious and grassy, and bearing all manner of fruits.

And when the boat touched the shore, we landed, and walked round about the island for fifteen days, yet could not reach the limits of it. No plant saw we there without its flower; no tree without its fruit; and all the stones thereon were precious gems. But on the fifteenth day we discovered a river flowing from the west towards the east, when, being at a loss what to do, though we wished to cross over the river, we awaited the direction of the Lord. While we thus considered the matter, there appeared suddenly before us a certain man, shining with a great light, who, calling us by our names, addressed us thus:

"Welcome, worthy brothers, for the Lord has revealed to you the land He will grant unto His saints. There is one-half of the island up to this river, which you are not permitted to pass over; return, therefore, whence you came."

When he had ceased to speak, we asked him his name, and whence he had come. But he said: "Why do you ask these questions? Should you not rather inquire about this island. Such as you see it now, so has it been from the beginning of the world. Do you now need food or drink? Have you been weighed down by sleep, or shrouded in the darkness? For the Lord Jesus Christ is the light thereof, and if men had not transgressed the commandment of God, in this land of delights would they always have dwelt."

Hearing this we were moved to tears, and having rested awhile, we set out on our return journey, the man in question accompanying us to the shore where our boat was moored. When we had entered the boat, the man was taken from our sight, and we went on into the thick darkness we had passed through before, and thus unto the Island of delights.

But when the brothers there saw us, they rejoiced with great joy at our return, as they had long bewailed our absence, and they said: "Why, O fathers, did you leave us, your little flock, to stray without a shepherd in the wilderness? We knew, indeed, that our abbot frequently departed somewhere from us and remained away sometimes a month, sometimes a fortnight, or a week more or less."

When I heard this I tried to console them, and said: "Brothers, harbour no evil thoughts, for your lives here are certainly passed at the very
gates of paradise. Not far away from you lies the island, called the 'Land
of Promise of the Saints,' where night never falls nor day closes; to there,
your abbot, Mernoc, resorts, as the angels of God watch over it. Do you
not know, by the fragrance of our garments, that we have been in the
paradise of God?"

They replied: "Yes, father, we knew well that you had been in the
paradise of God, for we often found this fragrance from the garment of
our abbot, which lingered about us for nearly forty days."

I then told them that I had abided there with my dear son, for a
fortnight, without food or drink; yet, so complete was our bodily
refreshment, that we would seem to others to have been filled to reple-
tion. When forty days had passed, having received the blessings of the
abbot and the brothers, I came away with my companions, that I might
return to my little cell to which I will go to-morrow.

Having heard all this, St Brendan and his brothers cast themselves on the
ground, giving glory to God in these words: "Righteous are You, O Lord, in
all Your ways, and holy in all Your works, who have revealed to Your children
so many and so great wonders; and blessed be You for Your gifts, who have
this day refreshed us all with this spiritual repast."

When these discourses were ended, St Brendan said: "Let us now proceed
to the refection of the body, and the 'new commandment'." When the night
was over, St Barinthus, receiving the blessing of the brothers, returned to his
own cell.

St Brendan sets sail with his companions

St Brendan soon after selected, from his whole community, fourteen monks.
Taking these apart, the venerable father Brendan retired with them into an
oratory where he addressed them as follows: "Dearly beloved fellow-soldiers
of mine, I request your advice and assistance, for my heart and mind are firm-
ly set upon one desire; if only it be God's holy will, I have in my heart
resolved to go in search of the Land of Promise of the Saints, about which
Father Barinthus spoke. What do you think? What is your advice?"

But they, well knowing the purpose of their holy father, replied, as with one
voice: "Father-abbot, your will is our will also. Have we not forsaken our parents? Have we not slighted our family prospects? Have we not committed into
your hands even our very bodies? We are, therefore, ready to go with you,

whether unto life or unto death, provided only we find such to be the will of God."

St Brendan and the chosen brothers then decided to make a fast of forty days, eating only every third day, and afterwards to take their departure. After those forty days, St Brendan, affectionately taking leave of his monks and commending them to the special care of the prior of his monastery, who was afterwards his successor there, sailed forth towards the west, with fourteen brothers, to the island where St Enda dwelt, and remained there three days and three nights.

Having received the blessing of this holy father and all his monks, he proceeded to the remotest part of his own country, where his parents abode. However, he willed not to visit them, but went up to the summit of the mountain there, which extends far into the ocean, on which is "St Brendan's Seat", and there he fitted up a tent, near a narrow creek, where a boat could enter.

Then St Brendan and his companions, using iron implements, prepared a light vessel, with wicker slides and ribs, such as is usually made in that country, and covered it with cow-hide, tanned in oak-bark, tarring the joints thereof, and put on board provisions for forty days, with butter enough to dress hides for covering the boat and all utensils needed for the use of the crew.

He then ordered the monks to embark, in the name of the Father, and of the Son, and of the Holy Ghost; but while he stood on the shore and blessed the little creek, three more monks from his monastery came up, and cast themselves at his feet, saying, "O dearest father, suffer us, for the love of Christ, to accompany you on your voyage; otherwise we will die here of hunger and thirst, for we are resolved to travel with you all the days of our lives."

When the man of God saw their great urgency, he ordered them to embark, saying: "Have your will, my children;" but adding: "I know well why you have come hither. One of you has acted well, for God had provided for him an excellent place; but for two others, He has appointed harm and judgement."

St Brendan then embarked, and they set sail towards the summer solstice. They had a fair wind, and therefore no labour, only to keep the sails properly set; but after twelve days the wind fell to a dead calm, and they had to labour at the oars until their strength was nearly exhausted.

Then St Brendan would encourage and exhort them: "Fear not, brothers, for our God will be to us a helper, a mariner, and a pilot; take in the oars and helm, keep the sails set, and may God do unto us, His servants and His little vessel, as He wills."

They took refreshment always in the evening, and sometimes a wind sprung up; but they knew not from what point it blew, nor in what direction they were sailing.

Their first discovery of land

At the end of forty days, when all their provisions were spent, there appeared towards the north, an island very rocky and steep. When they drew near it, they saw its cliffs upright like a wall, and many streams of water rushing down into the sea from the summit of the island; but they could not discover a landing-place for the boat.

Being sorely distressed with hunger and thirst, the brothers got some vessels in which to catch the water as it fell; but St Brendan cautioned them: "Brothers! Do not a foolish thing; while God wills not to show us a landing-place, you would take this without His permission; but after three days the Lord Jesus Christ will show His servants a secure harbour and resting-place, where you may refresh your wearied bodies."

When they had sailed round the island for three days, they saw, on the third day, about the hour of none, a small cove, where the boat could enter; and St Brendan immediately arose and blessed this landing-place, where the rocks stood on every side, of wonderful steepness like a wall.

When all had disembarked and stood upon the beach, St Brendan directed them to remove nothing from the boat, and then there appeared a dog, approaching from a bye-path, who came to fawn upon the saint, as dogs are wont to fawn upon their masters.

"Has not the Lord," said St Brendan, "sent us a goodly messenger; let us follow him"; and the brothers followed the dog, until they came to a large mansion, in which they found a spacious hall, laid out with couches and seats, and water for washing their feet.

When they had taken some rest, St Brendan warned them thus: "Beware lest Satan lead you into temptation, for I can see him urging one of the three monks, who followed after us from the monastery, to a wicked theft. Pray you for his soul, for his flesh is in Satan's power."

The mansion where they abode had its walls hung around with vessels made of various metals, with bridle-bits and horns inlaid with silver.

St Brendan ordered the serving brother to produce the meal which God had sent them; and without delay the table was laid with napkins, and with white loaves and fish for each brother. When all had been laid out, St Brendan blessed the repast and the brothers: "Let us give praise to the God of heaven, who provides food for all His creatures."

Then the brothers partook of the repast, giving thanks to the Lord, and likewise took drink, as much as they pleased. After the meal was finished, and the divine office discharged, St Brendan said: "Go to your rest now; here you see couches well dressed for each of you; and you need to rest those limbs overwearied by your labours during our voyage."

When the brothers had gone to sleep, St Brendan saw the demon, in the guise of a little black boy, at his work, having in his hands a bridle-bit, and beckoning to the monk before mentioned; then he rose from his couch, and remained all night in prayer.

When morning came, the brothers hastened to perform the divine office, and wishing to take to their boat again, they found the table laid for their meal, as on the previous day; and so for three days and nights did God provide their repasts for His servants

Afterwards St Brendan set out on his journey with the brothers, first cautioning them not to take away any property from the island.

"God forbid," said they, "that any of us should dishonour our journey by theft."

Whereupon St Brendan said: "Behold the brother of whom I spoke to you yesterday has concealed in his bosom a silver bridle-bit which the devil gave him last night."

When the brother in question heard this, he cast away the bridle-bit out of his bosom, and fell at the feet of the saint, crying aloud: "O father, I am guilty; forgive me, and pray that my soul may not be lost"; and all the brothers cast themselves on the ground earnestly beseeching the Lord for his soul's sake.

When they rose from the ground, and St Brendan had raised up the guilty brother, they all saw a little black boy leap out of his bosom, howling loudly: "Why, O man of God, do you expel me from my abode, where I have lived for seven years, and drive me away, as a stranger, from my secure possession?"

Then St Brendan said: "I command you, in the name of the Lord Jesus Christ, that you injure no man until the day of judgement." And turning to the penitent brother, he told him to prepare without delay to receive the body and blood of the Lord, as his soul would soon depart from his body, and that there would be his burial-place, but that the other brother who accompanied him from the monastery would be buried in hell. Soon after, the soul of the brother who received the Holy Viaticum departed this life, and was taken up to heaven by angels of light in the sight of his brothers, who gave him Christian burial in that place.

St Brendan and the brothers came to the shore where the boat lay and embarked at once; whereupon a young man presented himself to them, bearing a basket full of loaves of bread and a large bottle of water, and said: "Accept this blessing from your servant, for your have a long way to go before you obtain the comfort you seek; but this bread and water will not fail you from this day until Pentecost."

Under this blessing they sailed forth upon the ocean, partaking of food only every second day, while the boat was borne along in divers directions until one day they came within view of an island, not far off, towards which they sailed with a favourable wind.

They visit Sheep-Island, and celebrate the Easter festival

When the boat touched a landing-place, the man of God ordered all to disembark, he being the last to leave the boat. In making a circuit of the island, they saw great streams of water flowing from many fountains, full of all kinds of fish. St Brendan said to the brothers: "Let us here perform the divine office, and sacrifice unto God the Lamb without spot, for this day is the festival of the Lord's Supper." And they remained there until Easter Saturday.

In the island they found many flocks of sheep, all pure white, so numerous as to hide the face of the land. Then the saint directed the brothers to take from the flocks what was needful for the festival; and they caught one sheep, which, being tied by the horns, followed at their heels, as if it were tame; and he also told them to take one spotless lamb. When they had obeyed those orders, they prepared to celebrate the office of the next day; and there came to them a man with a basket of hearth-cakes and other provisions, which he laid at the feet of the man of God, prostrating himself three times, and saying, with tears: "Oh, precious pearl of God, how have I deserved this, that you should take food at this holy season from the labour of my hands."

St Brendan, then raising him up from the ground, said: "My son, our Lord Jesus Christ has provided for us a suitable place wherein to celebrate His holy resurrection."

Afterwards he proceeded to perform the "ministering to the servants of God" [the washing of feet] and to prepare what was needful for the morrow's festival. When the supply of provisions was taken into the vessel, the man who brought them said to St Brendan: "Your boat can carry no more now, but after eight days I will send you food and drink sufficient until Pentecost."

Whereupon the man of God said to him: "How can you know for certain where we will be after eight days?"

And he replied: "This night you will spend on that island you see near you, and tomorrow also until noon; then you will sail on to the island not far from it towards the west, called the 'Paradise of Birds,' and there will you abide until the octave of Pentecost."

St Brendan asked him also why the sheep were so very large on that island, larger even than oxen; and he told him that they were so much larger there than in the lands known to St Brendan, because they were never milked, and felt not the stress of winter, having at all seasons abundant pasture.

They then went on board their vessel, and having given and received parting blessings, they proceeded on their voyage. When they drew nigh to the nearest island, the boat stopped before they reached a landing place; and the saint ordered the brothers to get out into the sea, and make the vessel fast, stem and stern, until they came to some harbour; there was no grass on the island, very little wood, and no sand on the shore.

While the brothers spent the night in prayer outside the vessel, the saint remained in it, for he knew well what manner of island was this; but he did not wish to tell the brothers, lest they be too much afraid. When morning dawned, he told the priests to celebrate Mass, and after they had done so, and he himself had said Mass in the boat, the brothers took out some uncooked meat and fish they had brought from the other island, and put a cauldron on a fire to cook them.

After they had placed more fuel on the fire, and the caldron began to boil, the island moved about like a wave; whereupon they all rushed towards the boat, and implored the protection of their father, who, taking each one by the hand, drew them all into the vessel; then relinquishing what they had removed to the island, they cast their boat loose, and sailed away, when the island at once sank into the ocean.

Afterwards they could see the fire they had kindled still burning more that two miles off, and then St Brendan explained the occurrence: "Brothers, you wonder at what has happened to this island."

"Yes, father," said they; "we wondered, and were seized with a great fear."

"Fear not, my children," said the saint, "for God has last night revealed to me the mystery of all this; it was not an island you were on, but a fish, the largest of all that swim in the ocean, which is ever trying to make its head and tail meet, but cannot succeed, because of its great length. Its name is Jasconius."

The Paradise of Birds

When they had sailed beside the island, where they had already been, for three days, and reached the end of it, they saw towards the west another island, not far off, across a narrow sound, which was very grassy, well-wooded, and full of flowers; and they bore away towards its landing-place.

When they had sailed to the southern side of this island they found a rivulet flowing into the sea, and there they brought the boat to land. The saint ordered them to leave the boat and tow it up against the stream, which was only wide enough for its passage; and thus they towed it for a mile up to the source of the rivulet, the saint sitting on board the while.

After some consideration, St Brendan said to them: "Behold, my brothers, God has provided for us a suitable place in which to abide during the Paschal time; and if we had no other provision, this fountain would, I believe, serve for food as well as drink."

For the fountain was, in truth, a very wonderful one. Over it hung a large tree of marvellous width, but no great height, covered over with snow-white birds, so that they hid its boughs and leaves entirely. When the man of God saw this, he wondered why this immense number of birds was thus brought together in one assemblage; and the question grew so irksome to him that with tears he besought the Lord, on his bended knees, thus: "O God, who knows what is unknown, and reveals what is hidden, You see the anxious distress of my heart; therefore I beseech You that You would vouchsafe, in Your great mercy, to reveal Your secret in what I see here before me; not because of my own worthiness, but solely in regard to Your clemency, do I presume to ask this favour."

Thereupon one of the birds flew off the tree, and in his flight his wings had a tinkling sound like little bells, over to the boat where the man of God was seated; and, perching on the prow, it spread out its wings in token of gladness, and looked complacently towards St Brendan.

Then the man of God, understanding from this that his prayer was granted, addressed the bird: "If you are a messenger from God, tell me whence have those birds come, and why this concourse of them here?"

The bird at once made answer: "We are sharers in the great ruin of the ancient enemy, having fallen, not by sin of our will or consent, but, soon after our creation, our ruin resulted from the fall of Lucifer and his followers. The Almighty God, however, who is righteous and true, has doomed us to this place, where we suffer no pain, and where we can partially see the Divine presence, but must remain apart from the spirits who stood faithful.

"We wander about the world, in the air and earth and sky, like the other spirits on their missions; but on festival days we take the shapes you see, abide here, and sing the praises of our Creator. You and your brothers have been now one year on your voyage, and six more years' journeying awaits you; where you celebrated your Easter this year, there will you celebrate it every year, until you find what you have set your hearts upon, the 'Land of Promise of the Saints.'"

When it had spoken thus, the bird arose from the prow of the vessel, and flew back to the other birds.

On the approach of the hour of vespers, all the birds, in unison, clapping their wings, began to sing: "A hymn, O Lord, becometh Thee in Zion, and a vow shall be paid to Thee in Jerusalem" [Ps 64]; and they alternately chanted the same psalm for an hour; and the melody of their warbling and the accompanying clapping of their wings, sounded like a delightful harmony of great sweetness.

Then St Brendan said to the brothers: "Take bodily refreshment now, for the Lord has sated your souls with the joys of His divine resurrection."

When supper was ended, and the divine office discharged, the man of God and his companions retired to rest until the third watch of the night, when he aroused them all from sleep, chanting the verse: "Thou, O Lord, wilt open my lips"; whereupon all the birds, with voice and wing, warbled in response: "Praise the Lord, all His angles, praise Him all His virtues."

Thus they sang for an hour every night; and when morning dawned, they chanted: "May the splendour of the Lord God be upon us," in the same melody and measure as their matin praises of God. Again, at terce, they sang the verse: "Sing to our God, sing; sing to our King, sing wisely"; at sext: "The Lord hath caused the light of His countenance to shine upon us, and may He have mercy on us"; and at none they sang: "Behold how good and how pleasant it is for brothers to dwell in unity." Thus day and night those birds gave praise to God. St Brendan, seeing all this, made thanksgiving to the Lord for all His wonderful works; and the brothers were thus regaled with such spiritual food until the octave of the Easter festival.

At the close of the festival days, St Brendan said: "Let us now partake of the water of this fountain; hitherto we had need of it only to wash our hands or feet."

Soon after this the man with whom they had been three days before Easter, who had supplied them with provisions for the Paschal season, came to them with his boat full of food and drink; and having laid it all before the holy father, he said: "My brothers, you have here abundance to last until Pentecost; but do not drink of that fountain, for its waters have a peculiar virtue, so that anyone drinking thereof, though it seems to have the taste and quality of ordinary water, is seized with sleep, and cannot awaken for twenty-four hours."

After this, having received the blessing of St Brendan, he returned to his own place.

St Brendan remained where he was with his brothers until Pentecost, the singing of the birds being a delight ever new to them. On the feast of Pentecost, when St Brendan and the priests had celebrated Mass, their venerable procurator, or provider, brought sufficient food for the festival; and when they had sat down together at their repast, he said to them: "My brothers, you have yet a long journey before you; take, therefore, from this fountain vessels full of its water, and dry bread that may keep for another year, and I will supply as much as your boat can carry."

He then departed with a blessing from all; and St Brendan, eight days afterwards, got the boat laden with the provisions brought by this man, and all the vessels filled with water from the fountain. When they had brought everything down to the shore, the bird before mentioned flew towards them, and alighted on the prow of the boat; and the saint, understanding that it would make something known to him, stood still where he was.

Then the bird, in human voice, addressed him: "With us you have celebrated the Paschal time this year; you will celebrate it with us also next year, and where you have been in the past year on the festival of the Lord's Supper, there will you also be on the same festival next year. In like manner, you will celebrate the festival of the Lord's Pasch, as you did before on the back of the great fish Jasconius; and after eight months you will find the island of St Ailbe, where you will celebrate the Nativity of Jesus Christ."

Having spoken thus, the bird returned to its place on the tree.

The Island of St Ailbe

The brothers got the boat ready, and set sail forth into the ocean, while all the birds sang in concert: "Hear us, O God our Saviour, the hope of all the ends of the earth, and in the sea afar off."

After this St Brendan and his brothers were tossed about to and fro on the billows of the ocean for the space of three months, during which they could see nothing but sea and sky, and they took refreshment only every second day.

One day, however, an island came into view, not far off; but when they drew near the shore the wind drove them aside, and thus for forty days they sailed round about the island without finding a landing-place. The brothers meanwhile besought the Lord with tears that He would vouchsafe to help them, for their strength was almost exhausted because of their great fatigue; and when they had thus persevered in frequent prayer for three days, and in fasting also, at length they found a narrow creek fit to receive one boat, and beside it two fountains, one foul and the other limpid. When the brothers hastened to take some of the water, the man of God said to them: "My children, do nothing that may be unlawful. Take nothing here without the leave of the venerable fathers who are on this island, and they will freely give what you would take by stealth."

When all had landed and were considering in what direction they should go, there came to them an old man, wasted from extreme old age, whose hair was white as snow and his face pellucid like glass. He prostrated himself thrice, before he went to embrace the man of God, who, raising him up from the ground, embraced him, as did all the brothers, in like manner.. Then this aged man, taking the holy father by the hand, led him to the monastery, about a furlong distant, when St Brendan stood at the entrance, and asked his guide whose monastery this was, and who was its superior.

He put to him various questions in this way, but could get no reply, only manual signs, indicating silence with much gentleness. As soon as the holy father recognised that silence was the rule of the place, he cautioned his brothers: "Restrain your tongues from much talking, lest the monks here be scandalised by your foolish talk."

After this, there came forth to meet them eleven monks, in their habits and crosses, chanting the versicle: "Arise, you holy ones from your dwellings, and come forth to meet us; sanctify this place; bless this people, and vouchsafe to guard us, thy servants, in peace."

The versicle being ended, the abbot embraced St Brendan and his companions in due order, and in like manner his monks embraced the brothers of the holy man. When the kiss of peace was thus mutually given and received, they conducted them into the monastery, according to the custom in western countries; and the abbot and his monks proceeded to wash the feet of their guests, and to chant the "New Commandment".

Then he led them all into the refectory, in strict silence; and when they had washed their hands he gave them a signal to take their seats, when one of the monks, on a given signal, rose up and supplied the table with loaves of bread of marvellous whiteness and roots of delicious flavour. The monks had taken places at table alternately with their guests, in due order, and between each pair a whole loaf was served, when the ministering brother set before them also some drink. Father abbot, in much cheerfulness, pressed his guests:

"Brother, from the fountain, out of which today you wished to drink stealthily, make now a loving cup in gladness and in the fear of the Lord. From the other fountain of foul water, which you saw, are the feet of the brothers washed, for it is always tepid. Those loaves of bread which you now see before you, we know not where they are prepared, or who brings them to our cellar; but we know well that, by the free gift of God, they are supplied to us, as an alms, by some obedient creature of His; and thus is fulfilled in our regard the words of divine truth: 'Those who fear God want for nothing.'

"Here we are twenty-four brothers, having each day twelve loaves for our support, one loaf for two brothers; but on Sundays and great festivals the Lord allows us a full loaf for each brother, so that of what remains we may have a supper; and now, on your advent, we have a double supply; thus it is that from the days of St Patrick and St Ailbe, our patriarchs, for eighty years until now, Christ provides us with sustenance. Moreover, neither old age nor bodily infirmities increase upon us here, neither do we need cooked food, nor are we oppressed with heat or distressed with cold; but we live here, as it were, in the paradise of God. When the hours for the divine office and for Mass arrive, the lamps in our church, which, under God's guidance, we brought with us from our own country, are set alight, and burn always without growing less."

When the repast was over, and they had thrice taken some drink, the abbot gave the usual signal, and all the brothers, in great silence, rose from the table, giving thanks to God, and preceded the father to the church, at the door of which they met twelve other monks, who readily bent the knee, as they passed. Then St Brendan said: "Father abbot, why have not those monks dined with us?"

"For your sakes," said the abbot, "as our table could not seat us all together. They will now take their meal, for through God's holy will they shall want for nothing. We will now enter the church and sing vespers, so that the brothers who are now dining, may sing the office afterwards in proper time."

When vespers had concluded, St Brendan took heed of the structure of the church: it was a perfect square of equal length and breadth, and in it were seven lamps, so arranged that three of them hung before the central altar, and two before each of the side altars. All the altars were of crystal, and the chalices, patenas, cruets, and the other vessels required for the Divine Sacrifice were also of crystal. Around the church were ranged twenty-four benches, with the abbot's seat between the two choirs of monks in rows on either side.

No monk from either choir was allowed to intone the chant of the office, but the abbot; and throughout the monastery no voice was heard, nor any sound whatever; but if a brother needed anything, he went to the abbot, and on his knees made signs that he wanted something; and then the father wrote on a tablet what God had intimated to him to be needful for the brother.

While St Brendan was pondering all these things, the abbot said to him: "Father, it is now time to return to the refectory, that all may be done with day-light, as it is written: 'He who walks in the light, stumbles not.'"

So it was done, and when all things were completed in due order of the daily routine, all hastened with alacrity to compline. Then the abbot intoned the versicle: "Incline unto my aid, O Lord," invoking at the same time the Most Holy Trinity; and they subjoin the antiphon: "We have sinned; we have acted unrighteously; we have worked iniquity; Thou, O Lord Christ, who art all mercy, have pity on us. In peace unto the selfsame, I will sleep and take my rest"; and they proceed to chant the office of compline.

When the office had concluded, the brothers went to their cells, taking their guests with them; but the abbot remained with St Brendan, in the church, to await the lighting of the lamps. The saint asked the father abbot about the rule of silence they observed; how such a mode of intercourse in a community was possible to flesh and blood. The abbot, with much reverence and humility, replied:

"Holy father, I declare before the Lord, that during the eighty years that have passed since we came to this island, none of us has heard from the other the sound of the human voice, save only when we sing the praises of God. Among us twenty-four brothers, no voice is raised; but signs are made by the fingers or the eyes; and this is permitted only to the elder monks. None of us, since we came here, has suffered any infirmity of body or mind, such as may be fatal to mankind."

Upon this St Brendan said with many tears: "Vouchsafe, I beseech thee, father abbot, to let us know whether we are permitted or not to abide here."

The abbot rejoined: "You are not permitted, for such is not the will of God; but why do you ask me, when God had revealed to you, before you came to us, what you must do? You must return to your own country, where God has prepared for you, as well as for your fourteen companions, the place of sepulture. Of the other two monks, one will have his pilgrimage in the island of the anchorites; but the other will suffer in hell the worst of all deaths;" and these events afterwards came to pass.

While they were thus conversing, behold, as they looked on, a fiery arrow, passing in through a window, set alight all the lamps that hung before the altars, and passing out through the same window, left the lamps burning.

Then St Brendan inquired who would extinguish those lamps in the morning, and the abbot replied: "Come, and see the secret of all this: you observe those tapers burning in the vases; yet none of them is consumed, nor do they grow less, nor do any ashes remain in the morning, for the light is entirely spiritual."

"How," said St Brendan, "can a spiritual flame thus burn in a material substance?"

"Have you not read," said the abbot, "of the burning bush, near Mount Sinai, which remained unconsumed by the burning?"

"Yes," said the saint, "I have read of this; but what analogy has it to this case?"

When they had thus remained on watch until morning, St Brendan asked permission to depart from the island, but the abbot replied: "No, O man of God, you must celebrate with us the festival of our Lord's Nativity, and afford us the joy of your company until the Octave of Epiphany."

The holy father, therefore, with his brothers, remained until that time, on this Island of St Ailbe.

They visit other islands

When those festival days had passed, St Brendan, with the blessing of the abbot and all his monks, and with a supply of the necessary provisions, set sail into the ocean; and there the vessel, without the use of oar or sail, drifted about in various directions, until the beginning of Lent.

One day they saw an island not far off, and quickly made sail towards it; for they were harassed with hunger and thirst, their store of food and water having been exhausted three days before. When St Brendan had blessed the landing-place, and all had landed, they found a spring of limpid water, and herbs and vegetables of divers kinds around it, and many sorts of fish in the stream that flowed from it to the sea.

Then St Brendan said: "Brothers, God has surely given us comfort, after our wearisome labours. Take of those fish sufficient for your repast, and dress them on the fire, and gather also those herbs and roots which God has provided for His servants."

When this was done, they poured out some of the water to drink; but the man of God cautioned them: "Take heed, my brothers that you use this water in moderation." But the brothers paid not equal heed to this caution, for while some drank only one cup of the water, others drank two cups, and others again drank three of them; so that upon some of them there fell a sudden stupor, which lasted for the space of three days and nights; when upon others it befell only for one day and night.

But St Brendan prayed without ceasing to God for them, as they incurred this great danger through ignorance. When three days had passed, the father said to his companions: "Let us, my children, hasten away from this fatal place, lest greater evil befall you; the Lord had given you refreshment, but you have turned it to your detriment. Go forth, therefore, from this island, taking with you as much fish as you may want for a meal on every third day, until the festival of the Lord's Supper; and also one cup of this water for each man, with a like supply of the vegetables."

Having laden the boat with those provisions, as the man of God directed, they set sail into the ocean in a northerly course.

After three days and nights the wind ceased, and the sea became like a thick curdled mass, so great was the calm. Then the holy father said: "Take in your oars, and cast loose the sails, for the Lord will guide our boat whithersoever He will."

In this manner was the boat kept in motion for the space of about twenty days, until at length God sent a favourable wind; when they put on sail, and worked their oars also in an easterly direction, taking refreshment every third day.

On a certain day there came into view an island, like a cloud, at a distance; St Brendan asked the brothers whether they recognised it. On their replying that they did not, the holy father said to them: "I know it well, my children, for we were on it last year, on the festival of the Lord's Supper, and therein our good procurator abides."

Hearing this the brothers, in great joy, plied their oars vigorously, putting forth all their strength; but the man of God said to them: "Senseless you are thus to tire out your limbs. Is not the Almighty God the pilot of our vessel? Leave her, therefore, in His hands, for He will guide her course as He will."

When they drew near to the island, their procurator came out to meet them; and, giving glory to God, led them to the same landing-place where they had landed the year before, where he embraced the feet of St Brendan and all the brothers, saying: "Wonderful is God in His saints." Having finished the versicle, and everything being removed from the boat, he set up a tent, and prepared a bath for them, for it was the festival of the Lord's Supper; and he provided new garments for all the brothers, as well as for St Brendan, performing all other services to them as was his wont.

The brothers then celebrated with great diligence the festival of the Passion of our Lord, until Holy Saturday, when, all the offices and ceremonies of the day being ended, and the festival of the Lord's Supper being fully completed, the procurator said to them: "Go now to your boat, in order that you may celebrate the vigil of Easter, where you celebrated it last year, and also the day itself, until the hour of sext; then sail on to the Paradise of Birds, where you were last year, from Easter until the Octave of Pentecost. Take with you all you require of food and drink, and I will visit you on next Sunday week." And the brothers acted accordingly.

St Brendan, giving his blessing to this good brother, embarked with all his brothers, and made sail to another island. When they drew near to the landing-place they found the cauldron, which in their flight the year before they had left on the back of Jasconius. Then St Brendan, going on land, sang the Hymn of the Three Children to the close, and cautioned the brothers: "Watch and pray, my children, that you enter not into temptation; consider well, how the Almighty God has placed under us, without difficulty, this greatest monster of the deep."

The brothers made their vigils here and there over the island, until the morning watch, when all the priests said their masses until the hour of terce; but St Brendan, getting into the boat with the brothers, there offered to God the Holy Sacrifice of the Immaculate Lamb, saying: "Last year we celebrated here our Lord's resurrection; and I desire, if it be God's holy will, to celebrate it here also this year."

Proceeding thence they came to the island called the Paradise of Birds; and when they reached the landing-place, all the birds sang in concert: "Salvation to our God, Who sits on the throne, and to the Lamb"; and, again: "The Lord is God, and He hath shone upon us; appoint a solemn day, with shady boughs, even to the horn of the altar." Thus with voice and wing they warbled, until St Brendan and his companions were settled in their tent, where they passed the Paschal time, until the Octave of Pentecost.

The procurator already mentioned came to them, as he had promised, on Low Sunday, bringing what was needed for their sustenance; and in mutual joy all gave thanks to God. When they were seated at their repast, behold the bird before spoken of perched on the prow of the boat, spreading out and clapping its wings with a loud sound, like a great organ, and St Brendan knew that it wished to convey to him this message, which it spoke as follows:

"The Almighty and merciful God has appointed for you four certain places, at four different seasons of the year, until the seven years of your pilgrimage will be ended. On the festival of our Lord's Supper you will be each year with your procurator who is here present The vigil and festival of Easter you will celebrate on the back of the great whale; with us here you will spend the Paschal time, until the Octave of Pentecost, and on the island of St Ailbe you will remain from Christmas until the festival of the Purification of the Blessed Virgin Mary. After those seven years, through many and divers perils, you will find the Land of Promise of the Saints which you are seeking, and there you will bide for forty days; then will God guide your return to the land of your birth."

When St Brendan had heard this, he, with many tears, cast himself prostrate, as did also the brothers, giving thanks and praises to the great Creator of all things. The bird then flew back to its place on the tree, and when the meal was ended, the procurator said: "I will, with God's help, come to you again on Pentecost Sunday with provisions."

And with a blessing from all, he took his departure.

They are miraculously saved from destruction

The venerable father remained here for the appointed time, and then ordered the brothers to make ready the boat, and to fill all the water vessels from the fountain. When the boat was launched, the procurator met them in his boat laden with provisions, which he quickly transferred into the boat of the man of God; and, with a parting embrace, returned whence he had come; but the saint sailed forth into the ocean, and the boat was borne along for the space of forty days.

One day a fish of enormous size appeared swimming after the boat, spouting foam from its nostrils, and ploughing through the waves in rapid pursuit, to devour them. Then the brothers cried out to the Lord: "O Lord who made us, deliver us, Thy servants;" and to St Brendan they cried aloud, "Help, O father, help us;"

And the saint besought the Lord to deliver His servants, that this monster might not devour them, while he also sought to give courage to the brothers in these words: "Fear not, you of little faith; for God, who is always our protector, will deliver us from the jaws of this monster, and from every other danger."

When the monster was drawing near, waves of immense size rushed on before it, even up to the gunwale of the boat, which caused the brothers to fear more and more; but St Brendan, with hands upraised to heaven, earnestly prayed: "Deliver, O Lord, Thy servants, as You delivered David from the hands of the giant Goliath, and Jonas from the power of the great whale."

When these prayers were uttered, a great monster came into view from the west, and, rushing against the other, spouting flame from its mouth, at once attacked it. Then St Brendan spoke: "Behold, my children, the wonderful work of our Saviour; see here the obedience of the creature to its Creator: await now the end in safety, for this conflict will bring no evil to us, but only greater glory to God."

Thereupon the rueful monster that pursued the servants of God is slain, and cut up in their presence into three parts, and its victor returned whence it came.

Next day they saw at a distance an island wide and full of herbage. When they drew near it, and were about to land, they found the rearmost portion of the monster that was slain.

"Behold," said St Brendan, "what sought to devour you. Now, you make your food of it, and fill yourselves abundantly with its flesh, for you will have a long delay upon this island. Draw the boat higher up on the land, and seek out a suitable place to fix our tent."

When the father had selected a site for their tent, and the brothers had, in compliance with his direction, placed therein the requisite fittings, he said to them: "Take now, of this monster's flesh, sufficient provision for three months, as this night will its carcass be devoured by the great fishes of the sea."

The brothers acted accordingly, and took as much of its flesh as was needed; but they said to St Brendan: "Holy father, how can we live here without water to drink?"

"Is it more difficult," said the saint, "for the Almighty to give us water than to give us food? Go to the southern side of the island, and there you will find a spring of clear water and abundance of herbs and roots, of which you will take a supply sufficient for your wants."

And they found everything as the man of God had told them.

St Brendan remained on this island for three months, for violent storms prevailed at sea, and severe stress of weather, from hail and rain. The brothers went to see what had become of the remains of the great monster, of which the saint had spoken; and they found, where its carcass had lain, only its bones, as the father had told them; and when they mentioned this to him:

"If you needed to test the truth of my words," said he, "I will give you another sign; this night will a large part of a fish, breaking loose from a fisher's net, be cast ashore here, and tomorrow you will have your repast on it."

Next day they went to the place indicated, and finding there what the man of God had foretold, brought away as much fish as they could carry. The venerable father then said to them: "Keep this carefully, and salt it, for it will be much needed, as the Lord will grant calm weather today and tomorrow; and on the third day, when the turbulence of the sea and the waves have subsided, we will take our departure from this island."

The three choirs of saints

When the three days had elapsed, St Brendan ordered them to load their boat with the skins and water vessels filled from the fountain, and with a supply of herbs and roots also, as much as might be needful; for the saint, since he was ordained a priest, ate of nothing in which had been the breath of life. Having thus laden the boat, they set sail in a northerly direction. One day they saw an island afar off, when St Brendan said to the brothers: "On that island, now in view, there are three classes of people: boys, young men, and elders; and one of our brothers will have his pilgrimage there."

The brothers asked him which of them it was; but he was loath to tell. When, however, they pressed the question, and seemed grieved at not being told, he said: "This is the brother who is to remain on this island."

He was one of the monks who had come after the saint from his own monastery, about whom he had made a prediction when they embarked in their own country. Then they drew near to the island, until the boat touched the shore.

The island was remarkably flat, almost level with the sea, without a tree or anything that waved in the wind; but it was of wide extent, and covered over with white and purple flowers. Here, as the man of God had told, were three troops of monks, standing apart, about a stone's cast from each other, and keeping at this distance asunder when they moved in any direction. One choir, in its place, chanted: "The saints shall advance from virtue to virtue; God shall be manifest in Zion"; and then another choir took up the same chant; and thus they chanted unceasingly. The first choir was of boys, robed in snow-white garments; the second was of young men, dressed in violet; and the third of the elder men, in purple dalmatics.

When the boat reached the landing-place it was the fourth hour; and at the hour of sext, all the choirs of monks sang together the Psalm: "May God have mercy on us, and bless us", to the end; and "Incline unto my aid, O Lord;" and also the psalm, "I have believed, therefore have I spoken" with the proper prayer.

In like manner, at the hour of none, they chanted three other psalms: "Out of the depths I have cried to thee, O Lord"; "Behold how good and how pleasant it is for brothers to dwell together in unity"; and "Praise the Lord, O Jerusalem; praise thy God, O Zion". Again at Vespers, they sang the psalms: "A hymn, O Lord, becometh Thee in Zion"; "Bless the Lord, O my soul"; and "Praise the Lord, ye children; praise ye the name of the Lord"; then they chanted, when seated, the fifteen gradual psalms.

After they had finished this chanting, a cloud of marvellous brightness overshadowed the island, so that they could not see what was visible before; but they heard the voices, without ceasing, in the same chant until the morning-watch, when they sang the psalms: "Praise the Lord from the heavens"; "Sing unto the Lord"; and "Praise the Lord in His saints"; and then twelve psalms, in the order of the psaltery, as far as the psalm: "The fool says in his heart".

At the dawn of day, the cloud passed away from the island, and then the choirs chanted the three psalms: "Have mercy on me, O Lord"; "The Lord is my refuge"; and, "O God, my God". Again, at the hour of terce, they sang three other psalms: "Oh, clap your hands, all ye nations"; "Save me, O God, by Thy name"; and, "I have loved, because the Lord will hear the voice of my prayer", with the Alleluia. Then they offered the Holy Sacrifice of the Immaculate Lamb, and all received the Holy Communion with the words: "This Sacred Body of the Lord and the Blood of our Saviour receive unto life everlasting."

When the Holy Sacrifice was ended, two members of the choir of the young men brought a basket full of purple grapes, and placed it in the boat of the man of God, saying: "Partake of the fruit of the isle of the Strong Men, and deliver to us our chosen brother; then depart in peace."

St Brendan then called this brother to him, and said:

"Give the kiss of peace to your brothers, and go with those who are inviting you. I say to you, that in a happy hour did your mother conceive you, because you have deserved to abide with so holy a community."

St Brendan then, with many tears, gave him the kiss of peace, as did also the brothers, and said to him: "Remember, my dear son, the special favours to which God has preferred you in this life; go your way, and pray for us."

Bidding them all farewell, the brother quickly followed the two young men to the companies of the saints, who, on seeing him, sang the verse: "Behold how good and pleasant it is for brothers to dwell together in unity"; and in a higher key intoned the Te Deum laudamus ("We praise Thee, O God"); and then, when all had embraced him, he was admitted into their society.

St Brendan set sail from the island, and when meal-time came, he told the brothers to refresh themselves with the grapes they got on the island. Taking up one of them, and seeing its great size, and how full of juice it was, he said, in wonder: "Never have I seen or read of grapes so large." They were all of equal size, like a large ball, and when the juice of one was pressed into a vessel, it yielded a pound weight. This juice the father divided into twelve parts, giving a part every day to each of the brothers; and thus for twelve days, one grape sufficed for the refreshment of each brother, in whose mouth it always tasted like honey.

When those days had passed, St Brendan ordered a fast for three days, after which a resplendent bird flew towards the boat, bearing in its beak a branch of an unknown tree, on which there was a cluster of very red grapes, and, dropping it near the man of God, flew away. Then he said to the brothers: "Enjoy this feast the Lord has sent us"; and the grapes being as large as apples, he gave some to each of them; and thus they had food enough for four days, after which they resumed their previous fasting.

Three days after, they saw near at hand an island covered all over with trees, closely set, and laden with such grapes as those, in surprising abundance, so that all the branches were weighed down to the ground, with fruit of the same quality and colour, and there was no tree fruitless or of a different kind in the whole island. The brothers then drew up to the landing-place; and St Brendan, leaving the boat, walked about the island, where the fragrance was like that of a house stored with pomegranates; the brothers, the while remaining in the boat, awaited his return, and the wind laden with those odours blew towards them, and so regaled them with its fragrance, that they heeded not their long fast.

The venerable father found on the island six fountains, watering the greenest herbage and vegetables of divers kinds. He then returned to the brothers, bringing with him some samples, as first-fruits of the island: and he said to them: "Leave the boat now, and fix up your tent here; be of good cheer, and enjoy the excellent fruits of this land which God has shown to us."

And thus for forty days they feasted on the grapes, and herbs, and vegetables watered by those fountains.

After that period, they embarked again, taking with them some of the fruits of the island, and sailed along as the winds shaped their course, when suddenly there appeared flying towards them the bird called *Gryphon*. When the brothers saw it, they cried out to the holy father: "Help us, O father, for this monster comes to devour us."

But the man of God told them to fear it not, for God was their helper. And then another great bird came into view, and in rapid flight flew against the Gryphon, engaging it in a combat that seemed for some time of doubtful outcome; but at length, tearing out its eyes, it vanquished and slew it; and the carcass fell into the sea, in the sight of all the brothers, who thereupon gave thanks and praises to God; meanwhile the bird which gained the victory flew away whence it had come.

They went to the island of St Ailbe, to celebrate the Christmas festival, and afterwards, taking leave of the abbot, with mutual blessings, they sailed about the ocean for a long time, taking rest only at Easter and Christmas on the islands before mentioned.

Some wonders of the ocean

On a certain occasion, when St Brendan was celebrating the festival of St Peter, in the boat, they found the sea so clear that they could plainly see what was at the bottom. They, therefore, saw beneath them various monsters of the deep, and so clear was the water, that it seemed as if they could touch with their hands its greatest depths; and the fish were visible in great shoals, like flocks of sheep in the pastures, swimming around, heads to tails.

The brothers entreated the man of God to say Mass in a low voice, lest those monsters of the deep, hearing the strange voice, might be stirred up to attack them; but the saint said: "I wonder much at your folly. Why do you dread those monsters? Is not the largest of them all already devoured? While seated, and often chanting upon its back, have you not chopped wood, and kindled a fire, and even cooked some of its flesh? Why, therefore, should you fear those? For our God is the Lord Jesus Christ, who can bring to nought all living things."

Having thus spoken, he proceeded to sing the Mass in a louder voice, as the brothers were still gazing at the large fish; and these, when they heard the voice of the man of God, rose up from the depths, and swam around the boat in such numbers that the brothers could see nothing but the swimming fish, which, however, did not come close to the boat, but swam around at some distance, until the Mass was ended, when they swam away in divers directions, out of the view of the brothers. For eight days, even with a favourable wind, and all sails set, they were scarcely able to pass out of this pellucid sea.

One day, on which three Masses had been said, they saw a column in the sea, which seemed not far off, yet they could not reach it for three days. When they drew near it, St Brendan looked towards its summit, but could not see it, because of its great height, which seemed to pierce the skies. It was covered over with a rare canopy, the material of which they knew not; but it had the colour of silver and was hard as marble, while the column itself was of the clearest crystal.

St Brendan ordered the brothers to take in their oars, and to lower the sails and mast, and directed some of them to hold on by the fringes of the canopy, which extended about a mile from the column, and about the same depth into the sea. When this had been done, St Brendan said: "Run in the boat now through an opening, that we may get a closer view of the wonderful works of God."

And when they had passed through the opening, and looked around them, the sea seemed to them transparent like glass, so that they could plainly see everything beneath them, even the base of the column, and the skirts or fringes of the canopy, lying on the ground, for the sun shone as brightly inside as outside.

St Brendan then measured an opening between four pavilions, which he found to be four cubits on every side. While they sailed along for a day by one side of the column, they could always feel the shade as well as the heat of the sun, beyond the ninth hour; and after thus sailing about the column for four days, they found the measurement of each side to be four hundred cubits. On the fourth day, they discovered, on the south side, a chalice of the same material as the canopy, and a paten like that of the column, which St Brendan at once took up, saying: "The Lord Jesus Christ has displayed to us this great marvel, and has given us two gifts therefrom, in testimony of the fact to others."

The holy father then directed the brothers to perform the divine office, and afterwards to take refreshment; for they had taken none since they came in sight of this column. Next day they rowed towards the north, and having passed out through an opening, they set up the mast, and unfurled the sails again, while some of them held on by the fringes, or skirts, of the canopy, until all was right in the boat. When they had set sail, a favourable wind came on aft, so that they had no occasion to use the oars, but only to hold the sheets and the tiller. And thus for eight days were they borne along towards the north.

A volcanic island

When those days had passed, they came within view of an island, which was very rugged and rocky, covered over with slag, without trees or herbage, but full of smiths' forges. St Brendan said to the brothers: "I am much distressed about this island; I have no wish to enter it or even to approach it – yet the wind is driving us directly towards it, as if it were the aim of our course."

When they had passed on further, about a stone's cast, they heard the noise of bellows' blowing like thunder, and the beating of sledges on the anvils and iron. Then St Brendan armed himself all over his body with the sign of the Cross, saying: "O Lord Jesus Christ, deliver us from this malign island."

Soon after, one of the inhabitants came forth to do some work; he was all hairy and hideous, begrimed with fire and smoke. When he saw the servants of Christ near the island, he withdrew into his forge, crying aloud: "Woe! Woe! Woe!"

St Brendan again armed himself with the sign of the Cross, and said to the brothers: "Put on more sail, and ply your oars more briskly, that we may get away from this island."

Hearing this, the savage man, above mentioned, rushed down to the shore, bearing in his hand a tongs with a burning mass of the slag, of great size and intense heat, which he flung at once after the servants of Christ; but it did them no hurt, for they were protected by the sign of the Cross. It passed them at a furlong's distance, and where it fell into the sea, it fumed up like a heap of burning coals, and a great smoke arose as if from a fiery furnace.

When they had passed on about a mile beyond the spot where this burning mass had fallen, all the dwellers on the island crowded down to the shore, bearing, each of them, a large mass of burning slag, which they flung, every one in turn, after the servants of God; and then they returned to their forges, which they blew up into mighty flames, so that the whole island seemed one globe of fire, and the sea on every side boiled up and foamed, like a cauldron set on a fire well supplied with fuel. All the day the brothers, even when they were no longer within view of the island, heard a loud wailing from the inhabitants of it, and a noisome stench was perceptible at a great distance.

Then St Brendan sought to animate the courage of the brothers, saying: "Soldiers of Christ, be strong in faith unfeigned and in the armour of the Spirit, for we are now on the confines of hell; watch, therefore, and act manfully."

Judas Iscariot

On another day there came into view a large and high mountain in the ocean, not far off, towards the north, with misty clouds about it, and a great smoke issuing from its summit, when suddenly the wind drove the boat rapidly towards the island until it almost touched the shore. The cliffs were so high they could scarce see the top, were black as coal, and upright like a wall.

Here the monk, who remained of the three who followed St Brendan from his monastery, leaped from the boat, and made his way to the foot of the cliff, wailing and crying aloud: "Woe is me, Father, for I am forcibly torn away from you, and cannot return."

But the brothers, seized with a great fear, quickly drew off from the shore; and, lamenting loudly, cried to the Lord: "Have mercy on us, O Lord, have mercy on us!"

St Brendan plainly saw how the wretched man was carried off by a multitude of demons, and was already burning among them, and he exclaimed: "Woe is yours, unhappy man, who has made you so evil an end of your life."

Afterwards a favourable breeze caught the boat, and drove them southwards; and as they looked back, they saw the peak of the mountain unclouded, and shooting up flames into the sky, which it drew back again to itself, so that the mountain seemed a burning pyre.

After this dreadful sight, they sailed for seven days towards the south, and then St Brendan observed a very dense cloud, on approaching which there came into view what had the shape of a man, sitting on a rock, with a veil before him as large as a sack, hanging between two iron prongs; and he was tossed about like a small boat in a storm. When the brothers saw this, some thought it was a bird; others, that it was a boat; but the man of God told them to cease the discussion, and to steer directly for the place; where, on his arrival, he found the waves all around motionless, as if frozen over.

They found a man sitting on a rugged and shapeless rock, with the waves on every side, which, in their flowing, beat upon him, even to the top of his head, and in their ebbing exposed the bare rock on which the wretched man was sitting; and the cloth which hung before him, as the winds tossed it about, struck him on the eyes and on the forehead.

When the saint asked him who he was, for what crime he was sent there, and how he had deserved to suffer so great a punishment, he answered: "I am that most unhappy Judas, the most wicked of all traffickers; not for any deserving of mine, but through the unspeakable mercy of Jesus Christ, am I placed here. I expect no place for repentance; but through the forbearance and mercy of the Redeemer of the world, and in honour of His Resurrection, I have this cooling relief, as it is now the Lord's Day; while I sit here, I seem to myself to be in a paradise of delights, considering the agony of the torments that are in store for me afterwards; for when I am in my torments, I burn like a mass of molten lead, day and night, in the heart of that mountain you have seen.

"There Leviathan and his satellites dwell, and there was I when it swallowed down your lost brother, for which all hell exulted, and belched forth great flames, as it always does, when it devours the souls of the reprobate. But that you may know the boundless mercy of God, I will tell you of the refreshing coolness I have here every Sunday from the first vespers to the second; from Christmas Day to the Epiphany; from Easter to Pentecost, on the Purification of the Blessed Virgin Mary, and on the festival of her Assumption.

"On all other days I am in torments with Herod and Pilate, with Annas and Caiphas; and, therefore, I adjure you, through the Redeemer of the world, to intercede for me with the Lord Jesus, that I may remain here until sunrise tomorrow, and that the demons, because of your coming here, may not torment me, nor sooner drag me off to my heritage of pain, which I purchased at an evil price."

The saint then said: "The will of the Lord be done; you will not be taken away by the demons until tomorrow." And he asked him what meant that cloth in front of him. Judas replied: "This cloth I once gave to a leper, when I was the purse-bearer of the Lord; but as it was not my own, I find no relief from it, but rather hurt; those iron prongs on which it hangs, I once gave to the priests for supporting their cauldrons; and the stone on which I am sitting, I placed in a trench on a public road before I became a disciple of the Lord's."

When evening came, a multitude of demons gathered round in a circle, shouting: "Depart from us, O man of God, for we cannot come near our comrade unless you retire from him, and we dare not see the face of our prince until we bring back to him his pet victim; give us therefore, our prey, and keep it not from us this night."

The saint then said: "I protect him not, but the Lord Jesus Christ has permitted him to remain here this night."

The demons cried out: "How could you invoke the name of the Lord on behalf of him who betrayed Him?"

The man of God then commanded them in the name of Jesus Christ to do him no hurt until morning.

When the night had passed, at early dawn, when St Brendan was proceeding on his way, a countless multitude of demons covered the face of the deep, uttering dreadful cries: "O man of God, accursed be thy coming and thy going, for our chief has this night scourged us with cruel stripes, because we had not brought back his wretched captive."

"Not on us," said the saint, "but on yourselves shall those curses be; for blessed is he whom you curse, and accursed is he whom you bless."

The demons shouted: "He will suffer double punishment for the next six days, because you saved him from his punishment last night."

But the man of God warned them: "You have no power, neither has your chief, only whatever power God may give you; and I command you in the name of the Lord, that you increase not his torments beyond those you were wont to inflict before."

"Are you," said they, "the Lord of all, that we should obey your command?"

"No," rejoined the saint, "but I am the servant of the Lord of all; and whatsoever I command in His name, it is done, and I am His minister only in what He grants to me."

In this manner they pursued him with their blasphemies until he was far away from Judas; and they bore off this wretched soul with great rushing and howling.

The rocky island of the holy hermit

St Brendan afterwards made sail for some time towards the south, in all things giving the glory to God. On the third day a small island appeared at a distance, towards which, as the brothers plied their oars briskly, the saint said to them: "Do not, brothers, thus exhaust your strength. Seven years will have passed at next Easter, since we left our country, and now on this island you will see a holy hermit, called Paul the Spiritual, who has dwelt there for sixty years without corporal food, and who for twenty years previously received his food from a certain animal."

When they drew near the shore, they could find no place to land, so steep was the coast; the island was small and circular, about a furlong in circumference, and on its summit there was no soil, the rock being quite bare. When they sailed around it, they found a small creek, which scarcely admitted the prow of their boat, and from which the ascent was very difficult.

St Brendan told the brothers to wait there until he returned to them, for they should not enter the island without the leave of the man of God who dwelt there. When the saint had ascended to the highest part of the island, he saw, on its eastern side, two caves opening opposite each other, and a small cup-like spring of water gurgling up from the rock, at the mouth of the cave in which the soldier of Christ dwelt.

As St Brendan approached the opening of one of the caves, the venerable hermit came forth from the other to meet him, greeting him with the words: "Behold how good and how pleasant for brothers to dwell together in unity." And then he directed St Brendan to summon all the brothers from the boat.

When they came, he gave each of them the kiss of peace, calling him by his proper name, at which they all marvelled much, because of the prophetic spirit thus shown. They also wondered at his dress, for he was covered all over from head to foot with the hair of his body, which was white as snow from old age, and no other garment had he save this.

St Brendan, observing this, was moved to grief, and heaving many sighs, said within himself: "Woe is me, a poor sinner, who wears a monk's habit, and who rules over many monks, when I here see a man of angelic condition, dwelling still in the flesh, yet unmolested by the vices of the flesh."

On this, the man of God said "Venerable father, what great and wonderful things has God shown to you, which He has not revealed to our saintly predecessors! And yet, you say in your heart that you are not worthy to wear the habit of a monk; I say to you, that you are greater than any monk, for the monk is fed and clothed by the labour of his own hands, while God has fed and clothed you and all your brothers for seven years in His own mysterious ways; and I, wretch that I am, sit here upon this rock, without any covering, save the hair of my body."

Then St Brendan asked him about his coming to this island, whence he came, and how long he had led this manner of life.

The man of God replied:

> For forty years I lived in the monastery of St Patrick, and had the care of the cemetery. One day when the prior had pointed out to me the place for the burial of a deceased brother, there appeared before me an old man, whom I knew not, who said: "Do not, brother, make the grave there, for that is the burial-place of another."
>
> I said, "Who are you, father?" "Do you not know me?" said he. "Am I not your abbot?" "St Patrick is my abbot," I said. "I am he," he said; "and yesterday I departed this life and this is my burial-place." He then pointed out to me another place, saying: "Here you will inter our deceased brother; but tell no one what I have said to you. Go down tomorrow to the shore, and there you will find a boat that will bear you to that place where you shall await the day of your death."
>
> Next morning, in obedience to the direction of the abbot, I went to the place appointed, and found what he had promised. I entered the boat, and rowed along for three days and nights, and then I allowed the

boat to drift wherever the wind drove it. On the seventh day, this rock appeared, upon which I at once landed, and I pushed off the boat with my foot, that it might return whence it had come, when it cut through the waves in a rapid course to the land it had left.

On the day of my arrival here, about the hour of none, a certain animal, walking on its hind legs, brought to me in its fore-paws a fish for my dinner, and a bundle of dry brushwood to make a fire, and having set these before me, went away as it came. I struck fire with a flint and steel, and cooked the fish for my meal; and thus, for thirty years, the same provider brought, every third day, the same quantity of food, one fish at a time, so that I felt no want of food or of drink either; for, thanks to God, every Sunday there flowed from the rock, water enough to slake my thirst and to wash myself.

After those thirty years I discovered these two caves and this spring-well, on the waters of which I have lived for sixty years without any other nourishment whatsoever. For ninety years, therefore, I have dwelt on this island, subsisting for thirty years of these on fish, and for sixty years on the water of this spring. I had already lived fifty years in my own country, so that all the years of my life are now one hundred and forty; and for what may remain, I have to await here in the flesh the day of my judgement.

Proceed now on your voyage, and carry with you water-skins full from this fountain, for you will want it during the forty days' journey remaining before Easter Saturday. That festival of Easter, and all the Paschal holidays, you will celebrate where you have celebrated them for the past six years, and afterwards, with a blessing from your procurator, you will proceed to that land you seek, the most holy of all lands; and there you will abide for forty days, after which the Lord your God will guide you safely back to the land of your birth.

The Paradise of Delights

St Brendan and his brothers, having received the blessing of the man of God, and having given mutually the kiss of peace in Christ, sailed away towards the south during Lent, and the boat drifted about to and fro, their sustenance all the time being the water brought from the island, with which they refreshed themselves every third day, and were glad, as they felt neither hunger nor thirst.

On Holy Saturday they reached the island of their former procurator, who came to meet them at the landing-place, and lifted every one of them out of the boat in his arms. As soon as the divine offices of the day were duly performed, he set before them a repast.

In the evening, they again entered their boat with this man, and they soon discovered, in the usual place, the great whale, upon whose back they proceeded to sing the praises of the Lord all the night, and to say their Masses in the morning.

When the Masses had concluded, Jasconius moved away, all of them being still on its back and the brothers cried aloud to the Lord: "Hear us, O Lord, the God of our salvation."

But St Brendan encouraged them: "Why are you alarmed? Fear not, for no evil shall befall us, as we have here only a helper on our journey."

The great whale swam in a direct course towards the shore of the Paradise of Birds, where it landed them all unharmed, and on this island they sojourned until the Octave of Pentecost. When that solemn season had passed, their procurator, who was still with them, said to St Brendan: "Embark now in your boat, and fill all the water-skins from the fountain. I will be the companion and the conductor of your journey henceforth, for without my guidance you could not find the land you seek, the Land of Promise of the Saints."

Then, while they were embarking, all the birds of the island, as soon as they saw St Brendan, sang together in concert: "May a happy voyage under his guidance bring you safely to the island of your procurator."

They took with them provisions for forty days, as their course lay to the west for that space of time, during which the procurator went on before them, guiding their way.

At the end of forty days, towards evening, a dense cloud overshadowed them, so dark that they could scarce see one another. Then the procurator said to St Brendan: "Do you know, father, what darkness is this?"

And the saint replied that he knew not. "This darkness," said he, "surrounds the island you have sought for seven years; you will soon see that it is the entrance to it;" and after an hour had elapsed a great light shone around them, and the boat stood by the shore.

When they had disembarked, they saw a land, extensive and thickly set with trees, laden with fruits, as in the autumn season. All the time they were traversing that land, during their stay in it, no night was there; but a light always shone, like the light of the sun in the meridian, and for the forty days they viewed the land in various directions and they could not find the limits of it.

One day, however, they came to a large river flowing towards the middle of the land, which they could not cross over by any means. St Brendan then said to the brothers: "We cannot cross over this river, and we must therefore remain ignorant of the size of this country."

While they were considering this matter, a young man of resplendent features, and very handsome aspect, came to them, and joyfully embracing and addressing each of them by his own name, said: "Peace be with you, brothers, and with all who practise the peace of Christ. Blessed are they who dwell in Your house, O Lord; they shall praise You for ever and ever."

He then said to St Brendan: "This is the land you have sought after for so long a time; but you could not find it until now, because Christ our Lord wished first to display to you His divers mysteries in this immense ocean. Return now to the land of your birth, bearing with you as much of those fruits and of those precious stones, as your boat can carry; for the days of your earthly pilgrimage must draw to a close, when you may rest in peace among your saintly brothers. After many years this land will be made manifest to those who come after you, when days of tribulation may come upon the people of Christ. The great river you see here divides this land into two parts; and just as it appears now, teeming with ripe fruits, so does it ever remain, without any blight or shadow whatever, for light unfailing shines upon it."

When St Brendan inquired whether this land would be revealed to men, the young man replied: "When the Most High Creator will have brought all nations under subjection, then will this land be made known to all His elect." Soon after, St Brendan, having received the blessing of this man, prepared for his return to his own country. He gathered some of the fruits of the land, and various kinds of precious stones; and having taken a last farewell of the good procurator who had each year provided food for him and his brothers, he embarked once more, and sailed back through the darkness again.

When they had passed through this, they reached the "Island of Delights," where they remained for three days, as guests in the monastery; and then St Brendan, with the abbot's parting blessing, set sail in a direct course, under God's guidance, and arrived at his own monastery, where all his monks gave glory to God for the safe return of their holy patron, and learned from him the wonderful works of God, which he had seen or heard during his voyage.

Afterwards he ended in peace the days of his life, on the nones of July, our Lord Jesus Christ reigning, Whose kingdom and empire endure for ever and ever. Amen!

The Voyage of Brendan

by Denis Florence MacCarthy

I grew to manhood by the western wave,
　　Among the mighty mountains on the shore:
My bed the rock within some natural cave,
　　My food whate'er the seas or seasons bore:
My occupation, morn and noon and night:
　　The only dream my hasty slumbers gave,
Was Time's unheeding, unreturning flight,
　　And the great world that lies beyond the grave.

And thus, where'er I went, all things to me
　　Assumed the one deep colour of my mind;
Great nature's prayer rose from the murmuring sea,
　　And sinful man sighed in the wintry wind.
The thick-veiled clouds by shedding many a tear,
　　Like penitents, grew purified and bright,
And, bravely struggling through earth's atmosphere,
　　Passed to the regions of eternal light.

And then I saw the mighty sea expand
　　Like Time's unmeasured and unfathomed waves,
One with its tide-marks on the ridgy sand,
　　The other with its line of weedy graves;
And as beyond the outstretched wave of time,
　　The eye of Faith a brighter land may meet,
So did I dream of some more sunny clime
　　Beyond the waste of waters at my feet.

But angels came and whispered as I dreamt,
　　"This is no phantom of a frenzied brain—
God shows this land from time to time to tempt
　　Some daring mariner across the main:
By thee the mighty venture must be made,
　　By thee shall myriad souls to Christ be won!
Arise, depart, and trust to God for aid!"
　　I woke, and kneeling, cried, "His will be done!"

The wind had died upon the Ocean's breast,
　　When, like a silvery vein through the dark ore,
A smooth bright current, gliding to the west,
　　Bore our light bark to that enchanted shore.
It was a lovely plain—spacious and fair,
　　And bless'd with all delights that earth can hold,
Celestial odours filled the fragrant air
　　That breathed around that green and pleasant wold.

Such was the land for man's enjoyment made,
　　When from this troubled life his soul doth wend:
Such was the land through which entranced we strayed,
　　For fifteen days, nor reached its bound nor end.
Onward we wandered in a blissful dream,
　　Nor thought of food, nor needed earthly rest;
Until, at length, we reached a mighty stream,
　　Whose broad bright waves flowed from the east to west.

We were about to cross its placid tide,
　　When, lo! an angel on our vision broke,
Clothed in white, upon the further side
　　He stood majestic, and thus sweetly spoke:
"Father, return, thy mission now is o'er;
　　God, who did call thee here, now bids thee go,
Return in peace unto thy native shore,
　　And tell the mighty secrets thou dost know.

"Seek thy own isle—Christ's newly-bought domain,
　　Which Nature with an emerald pencil paints:
Such as it is, long, long shall it remain,
　　The school of Truth, the College of the Saints,
The student's bower, the hermit's calm retreat,
　　The stranger's home, the hospitable hearth,
The shrine to which shall wander pilgrim feet
　　From all the neighbouring nations of the earth."

He ceased and vanished from our dazzled sight,
　　While harps and sacred hymns rang sweetly o'er
For us again we winged our homeward flight
　　O'er the great ocean to our native shore;

And as a proof of God's protecting hand,
  And of the wondrous tidings that we bear,
The fragrant perfume of that heavenly land
  Clings to the very garments that we wear.

Sources

Adamnán, *Life of Saint Columba*, ed. W. Reeves, 1856, reprinted Lampeter, Dyfed, 1988.

Burgess, Glyn S., & Clara Strijbosch, *The legend of St Brendan: a critical bibliography*, Dublin, Royal Irish Academy, 2000.

de Paor, Liam, *Saint Patrick's world*, Dublin, 1996.

Farmer, D.H. (ed.), *The age of Bede*, London, 1998.

Healy, John, *Insula sanctorum et doctorum: Ireland's ancient schools and scholars*, Dublin, 1902.

Herbert, Máire, *Iona, Kells and Derry*, Oxford, 1988.

Little, George A., *Brendan the Navigator*, Dublin, 1945.

Mac Airt, Seán (ed.) *The Annals of Inisfallen*, Dublin, 1977.

Moran, Patrick, *Acta Sancti Brendani*, Dublin, 1872.

O Cróinín, Dáibhí, *Early medieval Ireland*, London, 1995.

O'Curry, Eugene, *Lectures on the manuscript materials of ancient Irish history*, Dublin, 1861.

O'Donnell, Manus, *The Life of Colum Cille*, ed. B. Lacey, Dublin, 1998.

O'Donoghue, Denis, *Brendaniana*, Dublin, 1893.

O'Hanlon, *Lives of the Irish saints*, Dublin, n.d.

Stokes, Whitley (ed.) *Lives of saints from the Book of Lismore*, Oxford, 1890.

Tommasini, Anselmo M., *Irish saints in Italy*, London, 1937.

Van Gennep, Arnold, *The rites of passage*, Chicago, 1909.